IF GOD IS IN CONTROL, WHY AM I A BASKET CASE?

Extraordinary Choices for a Joy-Filled Life

Debbie Taylor Williams

BIRMINGHAM, ALABAMA

New Hope® Publishers
P. O. Box 12065
Birmingham, AL 35202-2065
www.newhopepublishers.com

New Hope Publishers is a division of WMU®.

The Library of Congress has catalogued the earlier edition as follows:

Williams, Debbie Taylor.
If God is in control, why am I a basket case? / Debbie Taylor Williams.
p. cm.
ISBN-13: 978-1-59669-224-4 (sc)
ISBN-10: 1-59669-224-3 (sc)
1. Bible. N.T. Colossians--Textbooks. 2. Worry--Religious aspects--Christianity. 3. Christian women--Religious life. I. Title.
BS2715.55.W55 2009
227'.70071--dc22

2008041729

ISBN-10: 1-59669-337-1
ISBN-13: 978-1-59669-337-1

N124143 • 0911 • 1.5M1

DEDICATION

Dedicated to my sisters in Christ,
who yearn to live an extraordinary life for Christ

Father,

Thank You for the privilege of studying Colossians. Thank You for every verse that gives us a glimpse into Your love and holiness. Thank You for the warnings, encouragement, and instruction. I pray each sister who does this study will never be the same. Imprint Your heart on her mind and heart. In the name of our precious Savior. Amen.

"Set your mind on the things above, not on the things that are on earth. For you have died and your life is hidden with Christ in God."
—Colossians 3:2–3

CONTENTS

Acknowledgments 8

Welcome 9

Introduction 10

Week 1 THE BIG PICTURE 13

Week 2 STRESSED OR BLESSED? 21

Week 3 RUNNING ON EMPTY OR FILLED TO THE BRIM? 49

Week 4 PITIFUL OR POWERFUL? 77

Week 5 DOWN IN THE DUMPS OR REVELING IN CHRIST'S GLORY? 107

Week 6 WEARING YOUR WRONGS OR WEARING YOUR WINGS? 135

Week 7 ARE YOU KIDDING? 161

Week 8 BASKET CASE OR EXTRAORDINARY? 189

Tips for Leaders 221

ACKNOWLEDGMENTS

A special thank you to my friends at New Hope Publishers: Andrea Mullins, Joyce Dinkins, Kathryne Solomon, Jonathan Howe, Ashley Crafton, Kathy Caltabelotta, and Sherry Hunt. It's a privilege to serve God with you.

To my husband, Keith, what would I do without you? You are my love and best friend. Thank you a million times over for your prayers.

Taylor, Lauren, Chris, and Ali, you're the greatest son, daughter, son-in-love, and daughter-in-love for whom a mother could pray. Do you know how much it means when you call and say, "How's your writing going? I'm praying for you"? I love you with all my heart.

Linda and Vicki, I am so blessed to have you as sisters. Thank you for all of your prayers. I love you so much.

Cynthia, Jean, and Jeannie, you've done it again—prayed and proofed me through another study. I love you and thank God for you.

Sisters at women's Bible study and prayer team, thank you for being present each week for the pilot study and for your prayers. You mean the world to me.

Most importantly, to God our Father, the Lord Jesus Christ, and Holy Spirit. You continue to amaze me. I love You and praise Your holy name!

WELCOME

Sisters,

Welcome to *If God Is in Control, Why Am I a Basket Case? Extraordinary Choices for a Joy-Filled Life.* Thank you for joining me, whether you are studying on your own or with a small group. This study is a follow-up to other books the Lord has allowed me to write to address women's issues, including *If God Is in Control, Why Do I Have a Headache? Bible Lessons for a Woman's Total Health.*

Of everything I've written, I've had the best time delving into this study of Colossians. There are many reasons. First, Colossians is filled with doctrine that provides for deep study. Although it is short, God has packed *each verse* with important spiritual truths for us to understand and apply. Second, Colossians is practical. Its truths touch the everyday issues of our lives. It equips us to live the abundant life God offers us, even though we may sometimes feel like "a basket case," or feel like we can't take one more stress.

Whether your basket-case situation arises from a bad medical report, an argument with a spouse, someone getting a promotion for which you longed, another driver pulling in front of you, a child spilling milk for the umpteenth time, or a poor choice for which you are now suffering, you'll discover wise counsel in Colossians.

As we take God's Word to heart, may it be said of us as it was of Daniel, he "began distinguishing himself... because he possessed an extraordinary spirit" (Daniel 6:3).

To each who possesses the extraordinary Spirit of our Lord Jesus Christ, may your joy increase with every extraordinary choice you make. I pray you're richly blessed as you dig into each day's study and discover the extraordinary life to which He's called you. "We give thanks to God, the Father of our Lord Jesus Christ, praying always for you" (Colossians 1:3).

My Prayer

Heavenly Father, You see each woman who has opened this study.
As she approaches Your Word, fill her with Your knowledge, wisdom, and understanding.
Grow and mature her into a woman who lives an extraordinary life for You!
In Jesus's name. Amen.

Love, Debbie Williams

INTRODUCTION

Sisters,

In order to get the most out of your study, please read the following suggestions, historical background, and reference notes.

Suggestions

1. Each weekly lesson is divided into five days of study. Please set aside time each day to complete your lesson rather than try to do several days in one day. Colossians is a rich study. You'll enjoy the study more and get more out of it if you savor one day of study at a time.

2. The first week provides an introduction in which you'll do an overview of Colossians and select favorite verses from each chapter. As you do, consider memorizing the verses over the next several weeks. I can't tell you how much it has meant to me to have Colossians 3:1–3; 3:17; and other verses hidden in my heart.

3. At the end of each day's study, you'll find a section titled "What's in Your Basket?" where you're given the opportunity to apply what you've studied. There you'll find two baskets. One is titled "Basket Case" and the other "Extraordinary Life." They represent two different ways we can live. This is the portion of our study where we take God's Word from an academic study and allow the Holy Spirit to touch our hearts. If we skip this or rush through it, we fail to give the Holy Spirit time to speak to us and change us.

Historical Background and Reference Notes

4. Each day begins with a fictional historical introduction. It is the story of "Mary," a believer in Colossae, who is excited that Paul has written a letter to her church. She represents how we might think or feel at times. Her questions and thoughts might be ours. She's *not* one of the Marys in the Bible. She's a fictional character.

   The second character is Paul. Paul is the real biblical character. However, I've taken the liberty to imagine what some of his feelings and thoughts might have been as he sat under house arrest and wrote to the Colossian believers.

5. Many believe that Colossians was written during Paul's first imprisonment in Rome. During this time, he was kept in or near the barracks of the praetorian guard or in rented quarters at his own expense—for two years (Acts 28:30).

6. The church at Colossae is thought to have been founded by a believer named Epaphras, who was converted to Christianity during the three years Paul was in Ephesus. The church was mainly Gentile. Epaphras either visited Paul in prison or

was imprisoned with him (Philemon 23), during which time he reported on the conditions of the church.

7. Colossae was located about 100 miles east of Ephesus in the Lycus Valley. Colossae, Laodicea, and Hierapolis were almost in sight of each other. Laodicea and Hierapolis stood 6 miles opposite each other with the Lycus River flowing between them. Colossae was 12 miles north.

   William Barclay tells us in *The Letters to the Philippians, Colossians, and Thessalonians* that the valley was known for its earthquakes and for the chalk in the river, which—when accumulated—caused gleaming formations. Volcanic ground not covered by chalk provided pastureland where sheep grazed. Colossae was famous for its dye.

   At one time the three cities were of equal importance. However, over the years Laodicea became a prosperous political and financial center. Hierapolis became a great trade center, well known for its spa where thousands of people came to bathe in the hot springs.

   Colossae, though in control of the roads to the Cadmus mountain ranges, declined in prosperity. Though ruins of great buildings in Laodicea and Hierapolis can still be seen, nothing remains of Colossae. It was the least important town to which Paul ever wrote.

8. The main threat to the Christians at Colossae was Gnostic heresy. Heresy means deviant and false doctrine. A group of intellectuals dissatisfied with the simplicity of Christianity wanted to turn the gospel into a philosophy of religion. In Colossians, Paul countered the Gnostic heresy as well as Jewish legalism, which threatened the church.

   Although we may feel far removed from what our Colossian brothers and sisters faced, we're not. A person searching for spiritual inspiration today can select from the same Web site devotionals by Max Lucado, talks by the Dalai Lama, teachings from a Buddhist, prayers by a witch, or a chakra "spiritual energy" bracelet. We're in as much need of doctrinal truth and warnings as the Colossians.

The Heresy at Colossae

Following is how William Barclay summarizes the heresy at Colossae, in *The Letters to the Philippians, Colossians, and Thessalonians*. The heresy:

1. Attacked the total adequacy and the unique supremacy of Christ.

2. Denied that Jesus was equal to God and Creator.

3. Stated that matter was eternal and evil. The universe was not created out of nothing, but out of flawed matter.

4. Believed the spirit alone was good. The heresy suggested that if Jesus were the Son of God, then Jesus couldn't have had a flesh-and-blood body; He would have been a spiritual phantom who left no footprints on the ground.

The heresy also purported:

5. Since God was spirit and altogether good, He could not be the Creator, for He couldn't touch evil matter.
6. In order to get to God, people must know all kinds of secret knowledge and hidden passwords.
7. Based on the fact that all matter was thought to be evil, Gnostics might either practice self-denial with all kinds of laws and restrictions; or reject the moral law altogether, in which any immorality was justified.
8. Higher levels of spirituality were open to only the chosen few, creating a spiritual and intellectual snobbery.
9. There was an astrological element based on the ancient world's thought regarding the influence of the spirit of the stars and planets.
10. Every natural force—the wind, thunder, lightning, rain—had a demonic controller, who were in one-sense intermediaries to God and in another sense barriers to Him.
11. At least some place was given to the worship of angels, who acted as intermediaries between human beings and God.

Word Meanings

Please note that your study includes Hebrew and Greek word studies; when these key words are defined, they will be italicized with the specific definition for the respective word in quotes. For example:

> *Knowledge* here means "precise and correct knowledge; knowledge of things ethical and divine."

These definitions come from sources including Strong's *The Exhaustive Concordance of the Bible*, *Wuest's Word Studies from the Greek New Testament for the English Reader*, and Bible references noted.

Many blessings as you feast your eyes and heart on Colossians!

♦ WEEK 1 ♦

THE BIG PICTURE

We begin our study this week by looking at the big picture of Colossians. You will have the opportunity to scan the whole book, pick out your favorite verses, and begin identifying attributes of God to which you can cling in the basket-case moments of your life.

Though the following accounts are fictional, they reflect the historical setting 2,000 years ago.

♦ ♦ ♦

As the first hints of red and orange streaked the morning sky, Mary arrived at the well to draw water. Lowering her clay pot, she pondered, *Why would Paul write to us, only a small village and church?* Glancing at the sunrise, she quietly prayed, "Jehovah, when Paul's letter is read today, show me how I can live an extraordinary life for You."

♦ ♦ ♦

Stirred by the Holy Spirit, the Apostle Paul's mind raced with all that he desired to write to the believers at Colossae. *Little did I know — when I led the persecution against, including murdering Christians — God would one day use* me *to write letters to encourage believers!*

♦ ♦ ♦

Could the Apostle Paul have ever imagined we would glean from his insights some 2,000 years after he wrote to the Colossians?

DAYS 1–3: *God's Word to Believers*

Heavenly Father, I'm thrilled to be in Your presence today, studying Your Word! Teach me how to live an extraordinary life that glorifies You. In Jesus's name. Amen.

If you or I had been a fly on the wall 2,000 years ago, we likely would have seen Paul kneel in prayer before beginning his letter to the Colossians. Why might that have been the case? Paul's letter begins with a prayer in which we hear God's heartbeat for us. Over the next three days, we will read Colossians 1–4, to see the big brushstrokes of this masterpiece of godly wisdom. We'll discover what God wants us to know about His Son and see the beauty of His desires for each one of us. Then, in the following weeks, we will more closely examine each golden nugget of truth.

As you read Colossians this week, record major points and words of encouragement you find in each chapter.

For example: Colossians 1:2 **God extends His grace and peace to me.**

1. Colossians 1

____

____

2. Colossians 2

____

____

3. Colossians 3

____

____

4. Colossians 4

____

____

What's in Your Basket?

Basket Case

- Read the Bible occasionally
- Caught off guard when basket-case moments happen
- Living an ordinary life

Extraordinary Life

- Meditate daily on God's Word
- Daily equipped with God's Word
- Living an extraordinary life for Christ

♦ *Am I a basket case because I don't make time daily to replenish my mind and heart with God's Word?*

♦ *Do I fill my mind with worldly thoughts or fill my mind with God's truths?*

Thinking It Over

♥ Prayerfully open your heart before God. In what way is God prompting or impressing you?

____

____

Day 4: *Committing God's Word to Memory*

Father, thank You for the opportunity to delve into Your Word. Thank You that it is life to us—our new life in Christ! Help me do more than study it. Help me savor Your Word until it becomes a part of my being. In Jesus's name. Amen.

Over the next few weeks, you'll have the opportunity to *memorize* verses from Colossians. According to the following verses, what's the value of hiding God's Word in our hearts?

Psalm 119:11 ____

Psalm 37:31 ____

Psalm 40:8 ____

Tips for Memorizing God's Word

✔ Prayerfully ask God to show you which verses He wants you to memorize. Then, skim over Colossians and select one or several verses.

✔ To better understand the context for a particular verse, read the verses before and after it. Ask yourself, *Is the verse talking about trials or does it reveal a promise to which I can cling? Is it a message of hope or does it call me to a higher level of commitment?*

✔ Write the verse(s) in the spaces provided.

✔ Meditate on the verses throughout our study. As an example, let's use Colossians 1:17, "He is before all things, and in Him all things hold together."

Colossians 1:17 states that Christ existed before all things. In other words, things don't surprise Him. He knew that Adam and Eve were going to sin. He knew He would safely take Noah through the flood in an ark. He knew He would use Moses to lead the Israelites out of Egyptian slavery. In addition, the Scripture verse says, "In Him all things hold together." Meditate on how Christ is not only the Creator, but also the Sustainer of all things.

- ✔ Consider the difference that the verse makes to you. For instance, the difference Colossians 1:17 makes to me is that, when I feel things are falling apart, I remember that God is holding everything together—including me! I think of times He's held me, such as when I was diagnosed with ovarian cancer. And I think of ways He has held me together in the past week.

- ✔ Consider how the verse applies to other people. Colossians 1:17 reminds me to encourage others with the truth that God is holding all things together. This verse reminds me to pray for family and friends to trust God when they're shaken.

- ✔ Look for repetition, contrasts, or similarities, and then diagram or sketch the verse. For instance, in Colossians 1:17, I wrote the verse as:

He is BEFORE   all things,
And IN Him   all things
HOLD TOGETHER.

- ✔ Pray the verse. *"Lord, You are before all things and in You all things hold together. I worship and praise You!"*

- ✔ Write the verse and then carry it with you throughout the day. Take it with you in your car and purse. Read it several times a day and before you go to bed. If you're on the computer, email it to yourself and reread it several times a day.

- ✔ Put your verse to music. Make up a tune or sing the verse words to a familiar tune.

USE THE SPACE BELOW TO RECORD THE VERSE OR VERSES YOU'VE SELECTED TO MEMORIZE OVER THE COURSE OF OUR STUDY. PLACE A CHECK MARK BESIDE EACH VERSE WHEN YOU'VE SUCCESSFULLY MEMORIZED IT.

Verse: ______________________ Memorized: ______________________

Verse: ______________________ Memorized: ______________________

Verse: ______________________ Memorized: ______________________

Verse: ______________________ Memorized: ______________________

Verse: ______________________ Memorized: ______________________

____

____

Verse: ______________________ Memorized: ______________________

____

____

Verse: ______________________ Memorized: ______________________

____

____

As you gain confidence in memorizing Scripture, you may decide to memorize a whole chapter. Years ago, one of my friends, Pam Kanaly, challenged me to join her in memorizing Colossians 3. I can't tell you the blessing it's been to have those verses hidden in my heart. We each bought a small spiral notebook and illustrated or diagrammed each verse to help us memorize the chapter. You can choose to do whatever works for you; but rather than hesitate, why not begin today?

What's in Your Basket?

Basket Case

- I don't memorize Scripture.
- God's Word isn't always in my heart.
- I often miss God's will.

Extraordinary Life

- I memorize Scripture, which helps me not sin against God.
- God's Word is in my heart.
- I delight to do God's will.

♦ *Am I a basket case because I don't take time to memorize God's Word?*

♦ *Am I a basket case because I meditate on my problems instead of God's promises?*

♦ *Do I hide my sin—not God's Word—in my heart?*

♦ *Do I delight to do God's will or miss God's will?*

Thinking It Over

♥ Prayerfully sit at God's feet and open your heart to Him. Confess anything He's showing you that contributes to your basket-case moments. ______________________

____

____

♥ Ask God to give you an increasing desire, consistency, and ability to memorize Scriptures that will help you live an extraordinary life for Him.

____

____

____

♥ Repeat the verse you most need to memorize. Ask God to fill your mind and heart with it throughout the week.

____

____

____

DAY 5: *God's Attributes as Revealed in Colossians*

> Father, You are the Almighty, the Grand One who encompasses all of life and sustains everything by the power of Your Word. I exalt and praise You. Please help me know You better through this study. In Jesus's name. Amen.

If we want to live extraordinary lives for Christ, our desire must be as Paul's: to know Christ and the power of His resurrection. Since every book of the Bible reveals God in a unique way, we want to take advantage of gleaning new insights into His character as revealed in Colossians. Therefore, today, look back over chapters 1–4. As you do, focus your reading on ways Paul describes God the Father, Son, and Holy Spirit.

RECORD IN THE FOLLOWING SPACES WAYS PAUL DESCRIBES GOD THE FATHER, CHRIST, AND THE HOLY SPIRIT.

Scripture	**How the Lord Is Described**
Example 1:17	Upholder of all things
____________	______________________________
____________	______________________________
____________	______________________________

What's in Your Basket?

BASKET CASE

- An elementary knowledge of God
- A stagnant relationship with God

EXTRAORDINARY LIFE

- A growing, powerful knowledge of God
- An intimate, growing friendship with God

- ♦ *Am I a basket case because I have an elementary, instead of maturing, knowledge of God?*
- ♦ *Am I a basket case because my friendship with God is stagnant and not intimate and growing?*

Thinking It Over

♥ Prayerfully open your heart before God. Do you long to know Christ more intimately? Do you yearn to experience His power in the midst of your trying moments?

____

____

____

Weekly Wrap-Up

Where Am I? With which basket-case point do I most relate?

____

____

____

Where Do I Want to Be? To which aspects of extraordinary living is God calling me?

____

____

____

How Will I Get There? What golden nugget and/or verse do I want to remember to help me better handle my basket-case moments and live an extraordinary life?

____

____

____

Thinking of Others: What from this week's study do I want to share with someone to encourage or warn them?

____

____

____

◆ Week 2 ◆

STRESSED OR BLESSED?

As we delve deeper into Colossians, we discover that we don't have to live defeated, stressed lives. Rather, we can choose to experience God's blessings in the midst of trying circumstances and worldly stresses.

◆ ◆ ◆

> Walking to the window, Paul gazed at the first rays of dawn. "Assure them their faith in You is sufficient for their needs. Flood them with Your peace. Focus their hearts on the hope awaiting them in heaven." Pondering the mystery of the Holy Spirit and how Jesus likened the Spirit to the movement of the wind, Paul continued, "Move in each believer's heart as he or she hears this letter read, Lord."

◆ ◆ ◆

> Mary's life had not been the same since she had become a Christian. Anxious to hear Paul's letter, she nestled into the last available seat as the elder began reading.

◆ ◆ ◆

Day 1: *Our Identity in Christ*

> Father, as I study today, move in my heart in a fresh way. Open my mind to new truths so I live my life to Your glory. In Jesus's name. Amen.

Read Colossians 1:1–2.

Although we might tend to gloss over the first verses of Colossians 1, Paul's greeting is more than a casual, "Hi!" Join me as we absorb each word.

1. In what way does Paul identify himself? ______________________________

____

2. Whom does Paul credit for his calling and apostleship? ________________

____

Paul's Identity and Calling

Numerous times in Paul's writings, he states he is who he is by God's will. One of the first steps to becoming a victor in Christ rather than a victim of circumstances is to view life in the framework of God's will. Paul didn't blame those who imprisoned him as thwarting him from accomplishing God's will. With his gaze heavenward, he trusted God's will and continued to serve Him.

3. How do you see yourself? Do you see yourself as a person for whom God has a divine calling? If so, what is it? ____

____

4. How faithfully are you fulfilling God's will for your life? Are you determined, as Paul, to identify yourself with God and His calling for your life whether you're a single, married, stay-at-home mom; career woman; or caregiver? Are your decisions based on fulfilling God's calling in whatever situation you find yourself?

____

____

God has a calling and will for each of us, even as He did for Old and New Testament saints. God used Esther, Ruth, Naomi, Mary, Elizabeth, Mary Magdalene, Lydia, Priscilla, and others. God wants to use you too. An important step in moving from a basket-case mentality to a faith mentality is to recognize God's calling, even in the midst of difficult circumstances.

5. Whom does Paul include in greeting the Colossians? ______________________

____

Timothy was a young man the Apostle Paul met during his second missionary journey. Timothy's mother and grandmother were godly Jewish women who raised Timothy to know God. Through the years, Paul became Timothy's spiritual father, because Timothy's own father was not a believer.

6. Paul identifies himself as called by the will of God. In what other way does he identity himself?
   ❑ A victim of the Jewish religious system ❑ A victim of the Roman government
   ❑ An apostle of Jesus Christ

Imagine if you were under house arrest and not free to come and go as you please. Imagine if you had a guard with you at all times. Some of you may feel that way to an extent. Perhaps:

- You are having marital difficulties and have an overly dominant husband.
- You might feel sandwiched between caring for your children and providing care for aging parents.
- You may feel housebound with your small children, though you love them very much.

The amazing thing about Paul is, he isn't a basket case about his house arrest. He doesn't complain or bemoan his circumstances. Had I been Paul, I probably would have cried against the injustice of my imprisonment. No doubt I would have felt sorry for myself. Would I have even included God on my list of accusations, knowing He could have intervened and prevented my imprisonment?

7. Have you ever been in a situation where your faith was "half-baked"? You trusted God, but failed to stay in the holy oven of prayer long enough to offer yourself and circumstance to His will? For your eyes only, what was/is your circumstance?

____

____

God doesn't want us to be basket cases of despair. Rather, when moments of despair occur, He wants us to turn to Him and discover His sufficiency. Rather than drag bitterness, resentment, jealousy, or worry through the day, we can empty ourselves of these emotions and cares at Jesus's feet. We can live extraordinary lives by considering what God wants to teach us in our situations.

Pause right now. Ask God to give you a new perspective about your situation. Ask God to help you view your life not as a victim, but as one called by Him. Take any trash baskets of despair, hard feelings, or self-pity to Him and empty them at His feet. Trade your trash basket for a picnic basket over which you fellowship with Him. Go to God every day and let Him fill you with the fruit of His presence and Spirit. (See Galatians 5:22–23.)

Your prayer:

____

____

____

Paul understood his identity in Jesus Christ. His faith amazes me! How many men or women do you know whom, while arrested, write letters to encourage others? Paul was able to do so because of his confidence and trust in God.

8. Who do you think might have accused Paul, tempting him to think God could no longer use him? (See Zechariah 3:1; Revelation 12:10.) ______________________

____

No doubt, Satan, the "accuser of our brethren," fired flaming arrows of self-doubt and despair at Paul (Ephesians 6:16). Yet Paul extinguished them and continued to serve God—even as we can.

9. I pray that, whatever your circumstance, you resolve to imitate Paul. Though he had every reason to be depressed and despondent, he remained God's faithful servant.

Check the following possible reasons for Paul's confidence.

- ❑ He had a sense of purpose and calling from God.
- ❑ He placed his focus on God and others rather than himself.
- ❑ He *submitted* to God's will and purposes.
- ❑ He understood his identity in Christ and apostolic calling were intact, though he was under house arrest.
- ❑ He was aware that he was a mentor to Timothy and others regarding how to handle adversity.

What about you? Have you had a change of location, or a physical or mental change that's "thrown you for a loop"? Although initial shock and dismay are normal, you can be assured that God still has a plan and purpose for your life.

Reread Colossians 1:2.

10. How does Paul describe those to whom he writes? ______________________

____

Paul describes those to whom he writes in five ways: *saints*, *faithful*, *brethren*, *in Christ*, and *at Colossae*. Let's consider each in light of our identity. (These are important reminders of who we are and whose we are!)

Saints

First, Paul calls Christians saints or holy. His eye is on a truth I sometimes forget: I'm "separated to God." Later, in Colossians 3:12, Paul reminds us that, because we're holy, we should behave in ways that reflect God's holiness. Does that hit home with you?

As those separated to God, we can respond differently to our basket-case moments than those who don't know Christ. Our calling allows us to see our circumstances as opportunities to glorify God in a holy way.

Faithful

Paul refers to the Colossians as faithful. Although this can be a general term for believers, Paul uses it as a description of those being faithful to their heavenly calling. Yes, we fall under the category of faithful. The big question is: Are we being faithful day by day, not only on Sundays?

Brethren

Third, Paul identifies the recipients in the tenderest of ways. He calls them brothers. Although *brethren* can be a term for fellow believer, it's more than an impersonal title. It's a reminder that we're born of the same heavenly Father. Jesus calls us brothers and sisters (Mark 3:35). If you've never had an older brother, you do now! If you've been an only child, say hello to your brothers and sisters in Christ!

In Christ

In Christ is a term Paul uses when contrasting believers from those who are "in the world," or unsaved. Our position in Christ shouldn't be taken lightly. It's our salvation! Think this one through a little more. You are *in Christ*, saved, and secured for eternity!

At Colossae

Although we're heaven-bound, God uses us during our stay on earth as His representatives. That's all it is—a short stay. While here, we bear the titles of His Majesty's witnesses, lights, and ambassadors. The continuous offering of ourselves at His footstool each day is not optional. He commands us to do so. It should be our first act when our eyes pop open every morning and should be repeated throughout the day and night as needed. (See Ephesians 5:18: "Be filled with the Spirit.") This is important if we want to manage our basket-case moments in a godly way.

11. If you're a believer, thank God for placing you in Christ. Thank Him for your heavenly destination. Offer yourself to God. Ask Him to work in and through you.

____

____

If you're unsure whether or not you're a Christian, settle the issue today. Visit with a Christian and ask that person how you can be saved. Or visit my Web site, www.debbiewilliams.com, and click How to Know Jesus. Let me know of your decision to accept Christ as your Savior so I can rejoice with you, even as the angels rejoice (Luke 15:7).

Today we'll close with two words of greeting from Paul. REREAD COLOSSIANS 1:2 and record his two words of blessing.

____________________ and ____________________

Grace and Peace

◆ ◆ ◆

> As Mary heard the words, "Grace to you and peace from God our Father," her heart soared. "Yes, truly, You're a God of grace and peace," she praised her heavenly Father.

My heart soars in praise when I read "grace and peace from God." The world is searching for grace and peace. Christians have both. Although Paul often used the greeting, "Grace and peace to you," it wasn't a mindless greeting. Grace is "that which affords joy, pleasure, delight, sweetness, charm, loveliness, good will, loving-kindness, favour." God's sweetness, favor, and loveliness toward us is seen most fully in the Cross. However, He wants us to experience it every day. Are you?

Peace is another gift from God. *Peace* is "the tranquil state of a soul assured of its salvation through Christ, and so, fearing nothing from God and content with its earthly lot." How many Christians could you honestly say reflect God's peace? Why not commit right now to be one who *does* reflect God's peace?

The Apostle Paul is a shining example of one whose heart was filled with the awareness of God's grace and peace—even during his house arrest. What I'd label as a basket-case situation for a man accustomed to being in the throes of activity, Paul labeled as an *opportunity* to be used for God. God was able to use Paul in an extraordinary way, not only for the Colossians, but also for Christians throughout all generations.

As Paul chose to respond to his difficult situation in an extraordinary way, we can choose to respond to our situations in extraordinary ways. We can choose to respond in the Spirit rather than react in the flesh. We can choose to be those through whom God pours forth His sweetness, favor, and peace in the midst of our basket-case circumstances.

Without doubt, we're going to find ourselves in basket-case situations. We'll receive a call from the emergency room. The milk will spill for the umpteenth time. There'll be challenges at work. The dog will run off. Friends will call with needs. Our nation will go through trying times.

Jesus fully understands what it means to go through trials. He dealt day in and out with those who challenged Him. He faced those who wrongfully accused Him. He ultimately felt the sting of their whip on His holy back and the agony of nails driven into His outstretched hands.

Paul knew what it meant to go through daily trials. He was whipped, stoned, shipwrecked, and imprisoned. He could have shaken his fist at God and cried, "Why did you open prison gates for me once, but won't now?" Instead, Paul trusted God in his circumstances. The result? God used Paul to write a letter of encouragement to believers. Paul chose in whom to place his faith. We can do the same.

What's in Your Basket?

Basket Case

- Despair
- Frustration and anger
- Self-pity

Extraordinary Life

- Realize God has appointed me to serve Him in the midst of my circumstances
- Grace and peace
- Assured of God's love

♦ *Perhaps I'm a basket case because I base my identity and feelings on my circumstances rather than on who I am in Christ and His will for me.*

Thinking It Over

♥ 1. Prayerfully open your heart before God. Look over today's lesson. In what area has God spoken to you?

____

____

____

♥ 2. Confess if you find your identity more in your circumstances or relationships with others than in your relationship with Christ. Talk to God about your attitude and the worries of your heart. Remember, He extends His grace, His sweetness, toward you.

____

____

____

♥ 3. Ask God to fill your heart with His grace and peace. Ask Him to teach you to see your circumstances through His eyes so you can live an extraordinary life that glorifies Him.

____

____

____

♥ 4. Thank God for hearing your prayer. Walk into your day knowing you're in Christ's hands for life and He extends His grace and peace to you.

DAY 2: *Faith in Christ, Loving in the Spirit*

Father, as I study Your Word, teach me to recognize when I'm stressed and to turn my worries over to You. Help me be known for my faith in You and love for others. In Jesus's name. Amen.

◆ ◆ ◆

Paul rose from praying. The guard rose too. He'd become a Christian after watching Paul live out his faith.

◆ ◆ ◆

A warm feeling overcame Mary as she listened to Paul's words and to what he prayed for them.

READ COLOSSIANS 1:3–4, 8.

1. For whom did Paul pray? ______________________________

Circle the word *you* in your Bible. Had I been Paul, commissioned to spread the gospel, yet under house arrest, I would have been a basket case.

2. Rather than fret, what did Paul do? ______________________________

____

____

____

3. How often did Paul pray for the Colossians? ______________________________

____

I don't believe Paul woke in the mornings, said, "Bless all those You love, Lord," and went about his day with a furrowed brow and a worrisome gnawing in his stomach. "Pray always for you" does not mean Paul literally verbalized prayer every moment of his day. When Paul makes statements such as "pray always for you" or "pray without ceasing," he is stating that he lived in a state of communing with God. He lived what he taught in Philippians 4:6–7.

4. Even if you know Philippians 4:6, write it in the space below. As you write the words, picture God speaking them to your heart. ______________________________

____

____

____

Paul was a learned, devout man who managed his stress by going to God in prayer. In prayer, he voiced his concerns to the Father. In addition, he listened to God. Today, we know not only the spiritual, but also the physical and emotional benefits of prayer. As you read the following effects of constant, unmanaged stress, consider if "basket case" or "extraordinary life" better describes you. Consider why Jesus tells us to pray, not worry.

The Effects of Constant, Unmanaged Stress

Constant stress causes our adrenal glands to be on high alert and releases cortisol to meet the stressful challenges we face. Clinician Marcy Holmes explains the effects.

> Sustained high cortisol levels destroy healthy muscle and bone, slow down healing and normal cell regeneration,...impair digestion, metabolism and mental function, interfere with healthy endocrine function; and weaken your immune system.
> —Marcy Holmes, "Adrenal Fatigue—The Effects of Stress and High Cortisol Levels," http://www.womentowomen.com

Ouch! No wonder Jesus tells us to pray, not worry!

The Blessings of Prayer

> A Duke University medical team concluded after looking at 4,000 older adults "that even occasional private prayer and Bible study helped people live healthier and longer lives."
>
> —Clem Boyd, "The Health Benefits of Prayer," http://ilus2prshim.wordpress.com

Here is another perspective on stress:

> Stress happens. Although sustained stress is harmful to your health and "can contribute to insomnia, depression, anxiety, obesity, heart disease, depression and other problems," not all stress is bad. "Momentary (acute) stress may actually boost your immune system, promote longevity and help you meet life's challenges."
>
> —"Stress Isn't All Bad," *Mayo Clinic Women's HealthSource*, April 2005,

What's the answer? Is it to check out of life to avoid stress? No, but we should pray about our commitments. We should take our calendars and checkbooks to the Lord. We can ask Him what to eliminate or change to make our lives less stressful if our health and relationships are being affected adversely. Rather than react to stress with anger or worry, we can respond to stress at God's footstool. We can seek divine guidance for how to handle our stress.

Can you imagine Jesus trying to explain to His disciples the physiological benefits of praying? Knowing they would not understand, He simply instructed believers to take the following actions.

5. What did Jesus say not to do? ______________________________

Matthew 6:31 ______________________________

6. What did Jesus say to do? ______________________________

Matthew 6:33 ______________________________

____

Matthew 7:7 ______________________________

Paul models praying in response to stress rather than worrying. We can make that choice.

7. Which fills your mind: worry or prayerfully going to the Father and asking Him for your needs?

____

How do we "always pray," that is, pray without ceasing? I find myself often praying throughout the day. When I feel stressful, I kneel if possible. I go before the Lord and turn the worry into a prayer. When I can't be alone or kneel, I quietly speak to God about whatever is worrying me. When someone calls with a concern, I take it to God in prayer that moment rather than offer to pray for the person later. God gives us the wonderful invitation to come to Him any time, day or night. Are you accepting His invitation?

8. What worry or stress are you experiencing? ______________________________
____
____

9. Have you gone to God with your situation and asked Him how to handle it? For instance:
   - If you are trying to decide whether to work outside the home. and if so, full time or part time, have you asked Him? ❑ Yes ❑ No
   - Have you asked God to lead you to the position where He wants you? ❑ Yes ❑ No
   - When your children misbehave, do you get on your knees and ask the Comforter to show you the best way to discipline your children, knowing each child is unique? ❑ Yes ❑ No
   - If your parents can no longer care for themselves, do you ask God to guide you in how to best care for them? ❑ Yes ❑ No
   - If you're a caregiver, do you seek God's wisdom for how to take care of yourself while caring for your loved one? ❑ Yes ❑ No
   - If you have an addiction or ongoing sin habit, do you faithfully ask God to show you the way to overcome it? ❑ Yes ❑ No

10. Equally as important, after you pray, do you stay in God's presence with pen and paper in hand so you can record His words to you? Do you follow through with what He tells you? ❑ Yes ❑ No

11. Without faith it is impossible to please God. Are you praying with faith or without it? If you pray with faith but have a habit of reverting to worry when stressed, make it a practice to turn your worries into prayers. Soon the practice of prayer will replace your practice of worry. Believe it. It can happen!
    ❑ I pray without faith. ❑ I pray with faith.

Faith in Christ, Love for One Another

Reread Colossians 1:4.

12. Check the following two points Paul heard about the Colossian believers:
    ❑ Their fasting ❑ Their controversy
    ❑ Their faith in Christ Jesus ❑ Their love for all the saints

Paul recognized two strengths in the Colossians: their faith in Christ and their love for one another. As William Barclay, in *The Letters to the Philippians, Colossians, and Thessalonians*, points out regarding this passage:

> It is not enough simply to have faith, for there can be an orthodoxy which knows no love. It is not enough only to have love for men, for without real belief that love can become mere sentimentality. A Christian has a double commitment—he is committed to Jesus Christ and he is committed to his fellow-men.

13. How does Paul describe the believers' love? (Colossians 1:8) ______________________

____

In verse 8, Paul refers to the believers' "love in the Spirit." This is key to living an extraordinary life. In the world, we have trying relationships. How are we to manage? Galatians 5:16 gives the answer: We walk in love by the Holy Spirit.

◆ ◆ ◆

> Mary listened attentively to Paul's words. She sought to grasp what Paul meant by loving in the Spirit. By the way the elder read "Spirit," she understood he was speaking of a new source from which she could draw love: the Holy Spirit. The image of lowering her pot into a well and drawing from a deeper source helped her realize she could draw from the wellspring of the Holy Spirit dwelling in her.

◆ ◆ ◆

Loving in the Spirit

Loving in the Spirit is different from loving in our flesh. Just as our fleshly bodies are able to feel love, there is a deeper, more profound love: God's love. It's a love that flows from God, the author of love.

All people have a spiritual capacity. Which of the following best describes you?

Spiritually Dead Unbeliever   Spiritually Carnal Christian   Spirit-Filled Christian

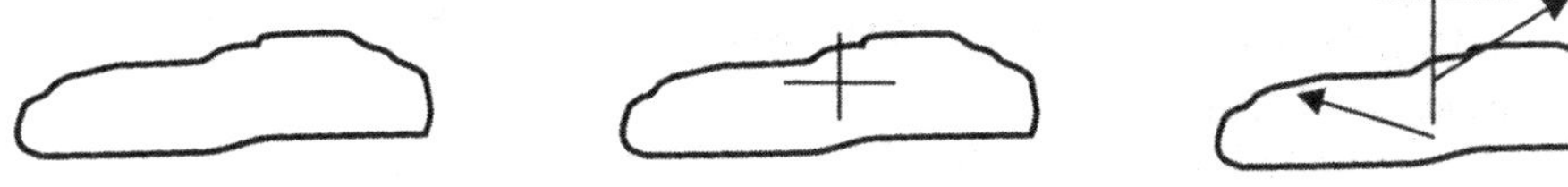

Spiritually dead people have the *capacity* to be filled with God's Holy Spirit. However, having denied Christ as Lord and Savior, *spiritually dead* people are void of God's Holy Spirit. Though they may attempt to fill their God-shaped vacuum with religious rites, nothing fits the God-shaped vacuum except Jesus Christ. Just as a wrong-shaped puzzle piece won't fit a puzzle, nothing but the Holy Spirit fits and fills our innermost being, for God created us for Himself.

A *spiritually carnal* Christian is one who has confessed his or her sin and accepted Christ as Savior. This person has been born of Christ's seed. The Holy Spirit is implanted in the soil of the person's innermost being for eternity. However, rather than watering God's seed through the Word and allowing Christ to grow in them, carnal Christians live by their natural, fleshly personalities.

A *Spirit-filled* Christian is a person who has professed faith in Christ, waters the Word implanted within them through obedience, prayer, and Christian service. The Spirit, in full bloom, fills that person's spirit. She or he bears the aroma of Christ's love, joy, peace, patience, kindness, goodness, faithfulness, gentleness, and self-control (Galatians 5:22–23).

Which are you? Spiritually dead, spiritually carnal, or Spirit-filled? Only when God's Spirit fills us are we able to love in the Spirit.

What's in Your Basket?

Basket Case

- Love in the flesh
- Worried and stressed

Extraordinary Life

- Love through the Holy Spirit
- Pray always in faith

♦ *Perhaps I'm a basket case because I respond to stress with worry rather than prayer.*

♦ *Perhaps I'm a basket case because I don't sit with God and quietly receive His instructions.*

♦ *Maybe I'm a basket case because I don't seriously approach God in faith. I pray because I know I'm supposed to pray, but don't really believe God's going to make all things right.*

♦ *Maybe I'm a basket case because there are people I don't like, much less love. Rather than seek the Spirit's filling, I hold to my bad feelings toward them.*

♦ *Perhaps I'm a basket case because, rather than ask God how to get off the stressful treadmill I'm on, I continue to live the same basket-case life day after day.*

Thinking It Over

♥ 1. What's in your basket? Are you moment by moment emptying your fleshly worries and stresses at Jesus's feet? Or, are you exhausted and angered by what's in your basket? ______________________________

____

♥ 2. Why not pray right now? Get rid of the emotional stress eating away at you. Prayerfully examine and confess the contents of your heart and mind. Pour out whatever is hindering your heart from living fully for God. ______________________________

____

♥ 3. Ask Christ to fill your heart with His Spirit so you know His will and mind. Ask Him to show you how to respond to your stressful situations. Listen quietly to how He guides you. ____

____

____

Day 3: *The Hope of Heaven*

Father, help me focus on the hope You've laid up for me in heaven when I'm faced with discouragement or difficulties. May my hope in You bring glory to You. In Jesus's name. Amen.

◆ ◆ ◆

Thinking on Paul's letter, "Grace and peace to you from God the Father," Mary rejoiced. A new sense of awe filled her as she pondered God's grace and peace toward her. In addition, she rejoiced that she was "in Christ." No one could snatch her from God's hand. For the first time, Mary began to realize God wanted to use her to bring others into His kingdom.

◆ ◆ ◆

Knowing the believers faced personal struggles as well as those who opposed Christianity, Paul searched for the words to encourage them. "If only they could get a glimpse of heaven, Lord." Thinking back to when he was caught up to paradise (2 Corinthians 12:2–4), he continued, "The hope of heaven; Lord help them grasp the reality of it!"

◆ ◆ ◆

Today many of us may be facing a difficult time. Physical, emotional, or financial problems may loom before us. I pray as you study today's lesson that you'll grasp the rich message of your hope of heaven. This world is not all there is. Yet, what we do with our time on earth is important. If you're a Christian, perhaps your troubled feelings come, as mine sometimes do, when I forget the hope of heaven. If so, I pray you're encouraged today.

Read Colossians 1:3–8. As you do, pay particular attention to verse 5.

1. Paul is an example of a committed Christian who's experiencing problems. He's also an example of keeping his eyes focused on the blessing unbelievers don't have. Paying particular attention to verse 5, check which of the following statements pertain to the Christian's hope.
   - ❑ The hope laid up for me in money, my children, a perfect marriage, and job
   - ❑ The hope laid up for me in heaven

Paul had a heavenly perspective. He framed every circumstance with it.

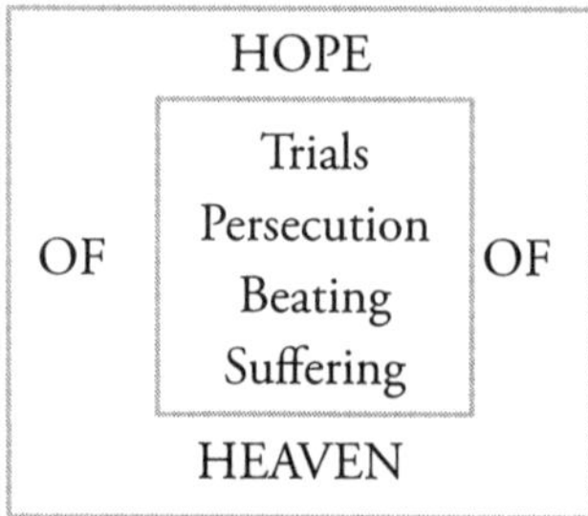

We do well to follow Paul's example. Rather than focus on dismal conditions or think *if only*... we can stay close to God in prayer. We can focus our hearts, as Paul did, on the hope laid up for us in heaven.

Is the hope a prize for which we must work? No. Paul explains it's "laid up" for us. Have you ever put something in layaway? If so, you understand what Paul's talking about. Christ paid for our salvation in full. He secured our heavenly hope when He died on the Cross for our sins. Our hope of heaven is in layaway for us.

2. Perhaps you're comforted knowing you'll go to heaven when you die, but right now you're struggling in the trenches of this world. Read the following, then record which aspects of heaven you look forward to the most.

John 11:21–25 ____

____

Revelation 21 ____

____

Revelation 22:1–5 ____

____

♦ *Perhaps I'm a basket case because I forget my heavenly hope.*

If you're going through a discouraging time, I pray you're encouraged as you focus the eyes of your heart on heaven. Perhaps you've lost a loved one, your husband's been unfaithful to you, or you're depressed. It may be you've fled an abusive situation, are alone, or don't know how you're going to make ends meet. God's blessing for you is His present help and the hope of heaven.

Gospel Truth

Paul reminds us of the truth of the gospel. Why? Because truth and lies often seem to run in the same circles. Wherever God is, Satan shows up. Disguised as an angel of light, Satan mixes a concoction of spiritual terms with deceptive phrases to lure unguarded souls into his lair. Some fall for his lies. Therefore, Paul clarifies that Christ is the only Savior and His gospel the only one that's true. What does Paul mean by "word of truth, the gospel"?

LET'S DO SOME EXPLORING INTO THE WORD OF TRUTH, THE GOSPEL. LIKE A MINER DIGGING FOR GOLD, LET'S DISCOVER WHAT LIES BENEATH THE ARCHAIC WORD WE SELDOM USE.

3. Look up the following ways *gospel* is used. Record who preached the gospel and what the gospel message is.

Scripture Reference	Who Preached the Gospel?	What Is the Gospel Message?
Mark 1:14–15		
Luke 9:1–2, 6		
1 Corinthians 15:1–5		

Gospel originally referred to a reward for good news, but later became the good news itself. Consider the following.

- The gospel is the good news of the kingdom of God. This is what Jesus preached. God has a kingdom in heaven and the saved will dwell in it.
- After Christ's death, the term included the message that Jesus suffered death on the Cross to gain our eternal salvation, was resurrected and ascended to the right hand of God in heaven, and will return in majesty to consummate the kingdom of God.
- The gospel is the narrative of the sayings, deeds, and death of Jesus Christ.
- The gospel is true. The word *gospel* is used more than 100 times in the New Testament. It was an important word Jesus often used. Therefore, it should be an important word to us. The gospel, or good news of the kingdom of God, is the best news we can share with others. It's the good news of the forgiveness of sins and heaven. Though some people say all religions are the same, simply different ways of getting to heaven, Christ says His message is the only *true gospel.*

4. With Christ's words in mind, read Colossians 1:6–7 then fill in the blanks.

   The gospel is for all the ______________________

   The gospel is constantly ______________ and ______________

   The gospel is learned from ______________________

Paul explained that the good news of Jesus isn't for a select group. It's for the world, is constantly bearing fruit and increasing, and is learned by faithful servants who share it with others.

5. How does Jesus affirm or disprove Paul's words in Matthew 24:14? ______

______

6. What other familiar verse in John explains that Christ came for the whole world, not a segment of it? ______

7. How does your belief that Jesus came for the world and is our only hope of heaven have an impact on your daily life and Christian responsibility? ______

______

8. The gospel increases and bears fruit. It's a work of the Spirit, but by what means is it spread? ______

______

9. What points from Romans 10:13–17 support the importance of teaching the gospel truth to others? ______

10. We know little about Epaphras except what we're told in Colossians 1:7. Record what we know. ______

11. Beloved, fellow bond-servant, faithful, servant of Christ, you learned from him describe Epaphras. Who do you know who fits that description? ______

______

Do you recognize that Christ is calling you to be that person (Matthew 28:18–20)? Why? Because Christ loves you and loves those who are not yet saved. He wants to use you to tell others about Himself. Christ is returning. The "end," as Jesus refers to it, is coming (Matthew 24:14). We who look forward to the hope of heaven have the privilege and responsibility to share Christ with the unsaved (John 14:6).

What's in Your Basket?

Basket Case

- Hopeless—Hope placed in people, money, possessions, self
- Unwilling to talk about Jesus to others

Extraordinary Life

- Hope placed in Jesus and heaven
- Sharing the gospel with others
- Fellow bond servants to others
- Faithful servant of Christ

- *Perhaps I'm a basket case because my hope is wrongly placed in people or things rather than in Christ and heaven.*
- *Perhaps I'm a basket case because I'm like a stagnant pond. I've received Christ, but I don't share Him with others.*
- *Perhaps I'm a basket case because I worry more about my temporal house than others' eternal homes.*

Thinking It Over

♥ 1. On a daily basis, what's on your to-do calendar? ______

______

______

♥ 2. How much of your schedule includes what God has placed there? ______

______

______

♥ 3. Why not prayerfully examine your daily basket? Consider getting up in the mornings and asking, *Lord Jesus, what do You want me to do today for You?* ______

______

______

♥ 4. If hopelessness and despair fill your heart, ask Jesus to fill your heart with the hope of heaven laid up for you. Ask Jesus to give you His eyes to see and ears to hear those who don't have the hope of heaven. Ask Jesus to fill you with a hunger for His Word so you're equipped and passionate to share the gospel. Tell Jesus you want to be a faithful, fruitful bond servant rather than be in bondage to your emotions, addictions, hobbies, or money.

Day 4: *Filled with the Knowledge of God's Will*

Heavenly Father, You are compassionate and unfailing in love. Fill me with the knowledge of Your will so I walk in a manner worthy of You. In Jesus's name. Amen.

♦ ♦ ♦

Mary woke with Paul's letter on her mind. Lying in bed, she pondered the inspired words and how God wanted to use them in her life. First and foremost, she determined to focus on Christ's grace, peace, and hope rather than others' faults. In addition, she determined to be more compassionate toward those who didn't know Christ and to speak of Him to others.

◆ ◆ ◆

Knowing the believers in Colossae received his letter, Paul fervently prayed for them. Peering into the night, he voiced his concerns to God, "Fill them with the knowledge of Your will in all spiritual wisdom and understanding so they walk in a manner worthy of You."

◆ ◆ ◆

Paul's Prayer

Colossians 1:9–12 is Paul's prayer for believers. Would you take off your shoes, slip on your sandals, and journey to Rome with me so we can eavesdrop on Paul as he prays?

Read Colossians 1:9–12.

1. For what does Paul pray? The believers be:
   ❑ Half-filled ❑ Filled

Filled

The word *filled* here means to "fill to the brim; supply liberally; to fill to the top: so that nothing shall be wanting."

2. To help you remember what *filled* means, record the definition in the space below.

____

____

3. With what does Paul pray we are filled to the brim?
   ❑ Money, success ❑ Good looks, prosperity ❑ The knowledge of God's will

How often do we say, "I just don't know what to do," regarding our marriage, children, finances, career, or church situation? God has a will for our lives and Paul prays we can be filled to the brim with it. In other words, God isn't asking us to play "hide-and-seek" with His will. Today we'll look at both knowledge and God's will.

Knowledge

Knowledge means "precise and correct knowledge; knowledge of things ethical and divine."

4. Rewrite Paul's sentence, inserting the definition of knowledge in place of the word *knowledge.* "We pray that you may be filled to the brim, liberally supplied with ______

____

Paul prayed we be filled to the brim, equipped with correct, ethical, divine knowledge of God's will. This is extremely important if we want to live extraordinary, not basket-case lives!

Consider, have *you* ever made poor choices because you lacked knowledge of God and His will? For instance, Christians have told me that if they had known God's teaching about marrying an unbeliever, they could've avoided much heartache. Parents tell me they wish they'd raised their children to know God's ways.

5. Knowledge of God and His will can be found through two sources. Thoughtfully meditate on the following, then record two ways we can know God and His will.

   Psalm 119:33–35, 38, 47–48 ____________________

   ____

   John 14:21, 26 ____________________

   ____

God has both a general will, given through biblical principles, and a specific will for us as individuals. The Bible and Holy Spirit work hand in hand to guide us into both. One will never negate the other. The more we know the Bible, the more the Holy Spirit can lead us in both God's general and specific will.

Paul prays for believers to be filled to the brim with a precise, correct, ethical, divine knowledge of God's will.

6. Bonus Question. Test your knowledge of God's general will. Choose one or several of the following and record His principle on the topic. Include the Scripture reference on which you base your answer.

   1) Marriage or singleness ____________________

   2) Child rearing ____________________

   3) Priorities ____________________

   4) Worry ____________________

Sometimes I wonder if God doesn't reveal more of His specific will because I'm not obeying His general will, which He's already given in the Bible. Might that be true of you?

God's Will

Often I think of my will rather than God's when I pray. Too many times "Thy will be done" is simply an attachment to the end of my prayer. How often when you wake in the mornings do you consider God's will for you? God knows the hours in your day. He knows what's going to take you by surprise. He knows Satan's schemes.

Sometimes we forget that God knows everything that's going to happen to us. He even knows our reactions. For example, consider when the Israelites fled Egyptian slavery. As you recall, Pharaoh hadn't wanted to let the Israelites leave. However, after the firstborn child in each Egyptian home died, Pharaoh told Moses, "Get out!" (Exodus 12:31–33). Why then, in Exodus 13:17, are we told, "God did not lead them by the way of the land of the Philistines, even though it was near; for God said, 'The people might change their minds when they see war, and return to Egypt.'" What war? Hadn't Pharaoh told the Israelites to leave Egypt?

God knew Pharaoh would change his mind, follow the Israelites, and war against them. Therefore, *God willed* that Moses lead the Israelites in a certain direction. Thankfully, Moses obeyed God! The result? God miraculously delivered the Israelites through the Red Sea, by which he also destroyed the Egyptians.

The same all-knowing God wants to lead us. He knows our today and tomorrows. He knows our enemy. Doesn't it make sense for us to follow His will?

Doesn't it make sense to study the Bible in order to know His general will? Shouldn't we take seriously the opportunity to pray to be filled with the knowledge of God's specific will?

- *Perhaps I'm a basket case; indecisive; overcommitted; in marital, child-rearing, or financial trouble because I spend too little time reading my Bible in order to know God's will.*
- *Perhaps we're basket cases because we wake in the mornings and hit the floor running without considering God's will.*
- *Perhaps we're basket cases because we ignore God's revealed general will.*
- *Perhaps we're basket cases because we don't pray about the "small stuff."*

We may not consider how our ordinary lives, in God's hand, are powerful to accomplish His will. However, a quick glance through Scripture will prove it to be so. Consider how God used:

- Noah's carpentry skills to build the ark
- David's skill with a sling to kill Goliath
- Orphaned Esther to save the Jews
- Young Mary to bear Christ
- Elizabeth to encourage Mary
- Demon-freed Mary Magdalene to run to the disciples with the good news of Jesus's resurrection.

God uses ordinary people who walk in His general will to accomplish His specific will. Though we may not see the big picture, let us pray to be instruments in our Master's hand.

Spiritual Wisdom

Paul prayed for believers to be filled with the knowledge of God's will. In addition, he prayed for believers to have spiritual wisdom and understanding. The word *spiritual* is significant. It defines the kind of wisdom we should seek.

7. What kinds of knowledge and wisdom are there other than spiritual wisdom?

___

We can be streetwise, money wise, smart in business. We can accumulate the wisdom of the world. However, the wisdom for which Paul prays is spiritual or divine wisdom. Think about that. Paul prays for you to have *divine* wisdom.

Do you know individuals whose intimacy with God enhances their ability to determine His will? Do you know those who are so intimate with God that their thoughts reflect His? This is the divine wisdom Paul prays we have.

The wisdom from above is different from worldly wisdom. Worldly wisdom falls short of divine wisdom.

8. How does James 3:17 define the wisdom from above?

1. ___ 5. ___

2. ___ 6. ___

3. ___ 7. ___

4. ___

Paul prays we be filled with the knowledge of God's will in all spiritual wisdom and understanding. Is his prayer being answered in you?

What's in Your Basket?

Basket Case

- Insufficient knowledge of God's will
- Lack of clarity
- Worldly wisdom

Extraordinary Life

- Filled with knowledge of God's will
- Divine clarity
- Divine wisdom

♦ *Perhaps I'm a basket case because I'm preoccupied with my will, not God's.*

♦ *Perhaps I'm a basket case who lacks clarity because I don't follow God's divine leading.*

♦ *Perhaps I'm a basket case who lacks spiritual wisdom because I spend more time becoming educated about politics, fashions, and finances, rather than spend time in God's Word.*

Thinking It Over

♥ 1. Go before the Lord and talk to Him about whatever's on your mind. Praise Him for His divine wisdom. ___

♥ 2. Repent and confess if you've not considered that your decisions are important to God. ______________________________

____

♥ 3. Tell your heavenly Father you would like to begin anew; you desire to live for His will. Open your heart. Ask the Lord to cleanse you of your past. Pray He fills you with His divine wisdom and the knowledge of His will. Commit to study the Bible so you grow in the knowledge of His will. ______________________________

____

♥ 4. Praise God for hearing you. Sing "Praise to the Lord, the Almighty" or "How Great Thou Art" or any words of praise to God. Celebrate that God has a will for your life!

Day 5: *Walk in Wisdom, Understanding, and Power*

Father, as I study Your Word today, quicken my mind and heart to consider how I can increasingly walk in wisdom, understanding, and power so I can glorify You in all I do. In Jesus's name. Amen.

◆ ◆ ◆

Paul woke thinking about what Epaphras told him regarding the believers' faith, progress, and challenges. The Colossians sought knowledge and spiritual insight. It was that very thing that caused Paul both joy and concern. Joy, because the believers were eager to grow. Concern, because false teachers abounded, offering false knowledge apart from Christ, while using Christian terms.

◆ ◆ ◆

Mary contemplated an invitation she'd received to attend a spiritist's talk at a friend's house. Apparently, the spiritist could tell people their future. While toying with the idea, Mary felt a nudge in her heart warning her to not go. Ignoring the nudge and assuring herself the woman's power must be from God, Mary headed to the meeting.

◆ ◆ ◆

Wisdom and Understanding

Today we conclude Paul's prayer for the believers at Colossae.

Reread Colossians 1:9–12, then answer the following questions.

1. In addition to praying for believers to have knowledge of God's will, for what more does he pray in verse 9? ______________________________

____

What's the difference between wisdom and understanding? *Wisdom* means "varied knowledge of things human and divine, acquired by acuteness and experience." It can be described as the knowledge of spiritual principles.

2. What does Paul partner with wisdom? ______________________________
____

According to Barclay, *understanding* here "is what the Greeks sometimes described as *critical knowledge*, meaning *the ability to apply first principles to any given situation which may arise in* life." When Paul prays for believers to have wisdom and understanding, he's praying we not only *understand* the great truths of Christianity, but we also *apply* them to everyday living.

In other words, it's not enough to have head knowledge of God's Word. We must take the great teachings of the Bible and apply them to our hearts and daily lives. We must connect the dots between what the Bible teaches about worry and how we actually respond when we're stressed. We must connect the dots between what the Bible teaches about child rearing and how we actually raise our children. We must connect the dots between what the Bible teaches about marriage and how we treat our spouse; between what the Bible teaches about difficult people and how we handle relationships.

Perhaps we're basket cases because we fill our baskets with spiritual teachings, but leave them at the church door rather than apply them when our child is upset with a coach, we're under financial pressure, our spouse angers us, we're at wits end with a co-worker, or despair looms like a black cloud.

Reread Colossians 1:10.

3. According to verse 10, what's the goal of knowledge, wisdom, and understanding?
____
____

Worthy

Worthy here means "suitably." Our Bible knowledge, spiritual wisdom, and understanding are meant to lead us to walk in a manner suitable of the Lord.

We know what it means to be suitable. A child who puts on dirty clothes for school is told to put on something suitable, something clean. Big question: How often do we consider if our actions, words, habits, or countenances are suitable to the Lord? Paul prays our knowledge, wisdom, and understanding result in walking in a manner worthy of the Lord.

4. What's the result of applying what we learn? We ______________________ Him in all respects (Colossians 1:10).

Have you thought about the fact that you can *please* God? We please God when we're filled with the knowledge of His will with all spiritual wisdom and discernment and walk in a manner worthy of Him. In other words, we please God when we know what He wants and we do it!

If I'm a basket case, perhaps it's because I'm more interested in pleasing myself than God. I may be a basket case because I want to please God, but I don't learn how to walk in a manner that pleases Him.

Bearing Fruit in Every Good Work

So far, we've looked at Paul's glorious yet practical prayer. In case you've been feeling, "I can't do all this," that's a normal response. That's why Paul asks God to do it! The things we've been studying are things Paul asks God to do! Let's recap.

Paul asks God to fill believers with the knowledge of His will in all spiritual wisdom and understanding so that they walk in a manner worthy of the Lord, pleasing Him in all respects.

Reread Colossians 1:10.

5. Complete the following sentence, indicating two results of knowing and walking in God's will; thus pleasing Him.
   ________________ fruit in every good work and ________________ in the knowledge of God.

Bearing fruit for God is our glorious privilege. Let's ponder the meaning of bearing spiritual fruit by considering what it means to bear children. Recently, as my husband, Keith, and I visited on the back porch, he suddenly asked, "Was it the most incredible thing in the world to have a human being growing inside you?" Then he continued, "What's it like now, to see Taylor and Lauren grown, and know they came from you?"

"Yes!" was my response, as I thought back to the first time I felt Taylor move within my womb. To experience the life of another human being within you is incredible!

Borrowing from the physical, we gain a glimpse of the awesome privilege of bearing spiritual fruit. Impregnated by the seed of Christ's Word and His Holy Spirit, we're able to bear spiritual fruit. We're able to experience Christ moving in us, bearing spiritual fruit through us when we're yielded to Him.

Perhaps we're basket cases because we know we're created for "more," but we ignore the One through whom the "more" is experienced.

6. What does 1 Peter 1:23 say about Christ's seed and you? ________________

____

7. What fruit do we have the privilege of bearing because we have Christ's seed? (Galatians 5:22–23) ________________

____

Even if we never bear physical children, we can bear spiritual fruit. We're designed to experience the awesome Spirit of God moving in and through us. Are we bearing or aborting God's fruit?

Increase in the Knowledge of God

We should be excited thinking about the opportunity to grow, bear spiritual fruit, and please God. As we look at this opportunity we may feel overwhelmed. We may say, "I don't have the power to live that kind of a Christian life. I've tried. I have the knowledge, but when it comes to applying it, I fail."

Meditate on Colossians 1:11–12.

8. In addition to a believer being filled to overflowing with knowledge, what more does Paul pray? To be strengthened with all ______________________________ .

Strengthened with All Power

9. Check the box below that most accurately describes the believer's power source.
   ❑ Our glorious might ❑ God's glorious might

Strengthen means "to make strong." Christians are able to apply God's principles not by our might, but by His glorious might.

Whenever I read a verse that refers to God's power or glorious might, I think back to when I first understood the difference between living by the Spirit and living by the flesh. It literally changed my life! (Galatians 5:16, 24–25)

10. When was the first moment you understood the difference between living by the flesh and living by the Spirit? ______________________________

____

What preceded your experience? ______________________________

____

What has life been like since that time? ______________________________

____

Perhaps if we're basket cases, it's because we live by our natural power rather than by the glorious, dynamic power of the Holy Spirit (Acts 1:8; Galatians 2:20; Romans 8:8–9).

Running on a low battery? Why not go to God's throne room and recharge in His presence? Be still. Be quiet. Let Him replenish you with His love. Let Him empower you as you rest in Him.

According to Colossians 1:11, what are the results of being strengthened with God's glorious power?

- ❑ Weakness
- ❑ Steadfastness
- ❑ Patience
- ❑ Joy
- ❑ Impatience
- ❑ Sadness
- ❑ Ungratefulness
- ❑ Thankfulness

We can go to our glorious Father first thing every morning and kneel before Him in worship and praise. We can ask God to fill us with His glorious Spirit so we can apply His spiritual principles throughout our day.

12. What blessings result when we do? Check the following you'd like to experience, as stated in the Scripture (Colossians 1:1–12).
    - ❑ We grow in the knowledge of God Almighty.
    - ❑ We're filled with a better understanding of His will.
    - ❑ We're empowered by His Spirit to walk in a pleasing manner worthy of the Lord.
    - ❑ We experience the joy of bearing fruit for Him.
    - ❑ We grow and increase in the knowledge of God.
    - ❑ We're strengthened with all power according to God's glorious might.
    - ❑ We attain steadfastness and patience.
    - ❑ We're joyful and thankful, mindful of all God has done for us.

God's blessings are not mundane blessings. They're blessings that result in right decisions that please Him.

We can't help but ask if we're basket cases because we don't grow in the knowledge of God, or if we grow in knowledge, we fail to apply that spiritual wisdom to our daily lives.

May each of us connect the dots this week between God's principles and applying them to our lives.

What's in Your Basket?

Basket Case

- Worldly knowledge
- Walk unworthily of the Lord
- Live by my might
- Please myself

Extraordinary Life

- Knowledge of God's will
- Walk by the Spirit
- Live by God's glorious might
- Please the Lord

♦ *Perhaps I'm a basket case because I'm not filled daily with God's glorious might. Perhaps I'm a basket case because I walk unworthily of the Lord rather than in a way that pleases Him.*

Thinking It Over

♥ 1. Which of the above baskets better describes you?

Although none of us can live an extraordinary life for God 100 percent of the time, He gives us the privilege of learning His ways and increasingly walking by His Spirit. Which of God's blessings have you, perhaps, been missing out on?

♥ 2. Praise God for His tender patience and love toward you.

♥ 3. Repent and confess anything in your heart that is displeasing to God.

♥ 4. Ask God to quicken your heart to crave His Word and apply it.

♥ 5. Ask God to teach you the difference between walking in the flesh in your strength and walking in the Spirit by His glorious might.

When God answers our request to discern increasingly between when we're walking in the flesh instead of the Spirit, we often don't like what we see of ourselves. Rather than beat ourselves up and feel guilty, let's instead thank God for showing us the difference. We can then repent and practice yielding to God. Learning to walk by the Spirit helps us increasingly please Him in all respects!

Living an extraordinary life is not living a perfect life. Only Jesus lived a perfect life. Living an extraordinary life doesn't mean we won't have basket-case moments. However, by growing in the knowledge of God and walking in His wisdom, understanding, and power, we can avoid some basket-case moments. In the midst of unavoidable basket-case moments, we can love in the Spirit and point others to the hope of heaven.

Weekly Wrap-Up

Where Am I? With which basket-case point do I most relate?

____

____

____

Where Do I Want to Be? To which aspects of extraordinary living is God calling me?

____

____

____

How Will I Get There? What golden nugget and/or verse do I want to remember to help me better handle my basket-case moments and live an extraordinary life?

____

____

____

Thinking of Others: What from this week's study do I want to share with someone to encourage or warn them?

____

____

____

◆ WEEK 3 ◆

RUNNING ON EMPTY OR FILLED TO THE BRIM?

This week we're going to discover the richness of our inheritance in Christ. Get ready to fill your heart with all that is yours in Him.

◆ ◆ ◆

Mary walked home from her friend's house with a heavy heart. She had been curious about spiritists and had therefore accepted Rachel's invitation to the "Embracing Your Angelic Mediator" lecture. Her excuse was she desired to have all God wanted for her. If she was honest with herself, however, she went because she was curious. Rather than wait for God to unfold her future, she wanted quick answers to her questions. Would she get married? Would her little brother get well? As the "spirit guide" led her through a reflective mantra, Mary became increasingly uneasy. In her spirit, she knew true knowledge and enlightenment come from God and His Word. Mary vowed never to return to the spiritists, but rather to walk daily in *God's* Light.

◆ ◆ ◆

Paul, having lived in Ephesus, was accustomed to false teachings. He knew what believers faced. Merchants carried not only their goods through the Lycus Valley, but also their mystic religions. Whether at the well or market, discussions often devalued Christ as Savior and led ungrounded seekers away from Christ, the source of true knowledge.

◆ ◆ ◆

Kneeling before the Father, Paul prayed. "Thank You for the true Light, Jesus. Thank You for qualifying us to share in the inheritance of the saints in light. Thank You for rescuing us from the domain of darkness and transferring us to the kingdom of Your beloved Son. Thank You for redeeming us and forgiving our sins."

◆ ◆ ◆

Day 1: *God Qualified Me*

Father, as I study Your Word today, flood my soul with a keen awareness of all You've done for me. Confirm Your Word in me so that I am quick to reject false teachings and follow only You. In Your name, I pray. Amen.

Read Colossians 1:12–14.

Last week we studied Paul's greeting and a large portion of his prayer for the Colossians. As you may have noticed, Paul's letter and prayer aren't written systematically. In other words, he didn't sit down and outline the topics he wanted to cover and the order in which he would present them. Therefore, when we study Colossians, we're reading his thoughts as they flow from his heart.

This week we'll look at the last points of Paul's prayer for believers. We'll begin by studying what God the Father did for us. Then, we'll examine arguments that were made against Christ's deity—arguments made not only in Paul's day, but also in ours. We'll discover that, although society offers ways to achieve peace apart from Christ, true peace with God is found in Jesus alone.

Reread Colossians 1:9–14, paying particular attention to our focal verses, 12–14.

Paul prays these specifics:

- He asks God's forgiveness of sins
- He gives thanks for the Colossians' faith
- He gives thanks to the Father

1. For what does Paul thank God? ____

____

Paul's spiritual understanding is so deep that his prayers flow with knowledge about God and Jesus. We rejoice in the following aspects of our salvation that we're reminded of in his prayer.

God Made Me Fit

Qualified here means "made sufficient, rendered fit." The verb *qualified* is used only one other time in the New Testament—2 Corinthians 3:6.

2. For what did God qualify and render you fit? ______________________________________

____

We certainly understand the concept of fit and unfit. For instance, it doesn't "fit" for a child with muddy clothes to romp on a neighbor's white couch. Prior to being washed of our sins, we weren't "fit" for God's kingdom. The following, though humorous, illustrates our unfit state.

MANUFACTURER'S RECALL NOTICE

Regardless of Make or Year or Tithe Amount, all units known as "human beings" are being recalled by the Manufacturer. This is due to a malfunction in the original prototype units code named "Adam" and "Eve," resulting in the reproduction of the same defect in all subsequent units. This defect is technically termed "Serious Internal Non-morality," but more commonly known as "SIN."

Symptoms of the SIN defect include, but are not limited to:

A) Loss of direction
B) Lack of peace and joy
C) Depression
D) Foul vocal emissions
E) Selfishness
F) Ingratitude
G) Fearfulness
H) Rebellion
I) Jealousy

The Manufacturer is providing factory authorized repair service FREE of charge to correct the SIN defect. The Repair Technician, Jesus Christ, has most generously offered to bear the entire burden of the staggering cost of these repairs. To repeat…There is no fee required. The number to call for repair in all areas is P-R-A-Y-E-R

Once connected, please upload the burden of SIN through the REPENTANCE procedure. Next, download ATONEMENT from the Repair Technician, Christ, into the SOUL component of the human unit. No matter how big or small the SIN defect is, Christ will replace it with:

A) Love
B) Joy
C) Peace
D) Kindness
E) Goodness
F) Faithfulness
G) Gentleness
H) Patience
I) Self-Control
J) Everything He Has Is Yours

Please see the Operating Manual, HOLY BIBLE, for further details on the use of these fixes. As an added upgrade, the Manufacturer has made available to all repaired units a facility enabling direct monitoring assistance from the resident Maintenance Technician, THE HOLY SPIRIT.

Repaired units need only make Him welcome and accept his Word and He will take up residence on the premises.

Source: Jeena Manoj. Used by permission of ICBS, Inc., publisher of 1stholistic.com and holisticonline.com.

Although we may smile at the preceding illustration, the message is true. God created Adam and Eve in His image. However, free will demonstrated a sin defect making us unfit for God's presence. God now makes us fit through Jesus, who took our sins and who, through the Holy Spirit, now indwells us.

Inheritance of the Saints

The good news is, God qualified us to share in the inheritance with other believers. What was on Paul's mind when he referred to our inheritance with the saints? Is he talking about earthly money? No. He has a wealth of more lasting value in mind. Probably two thoughts were on Paul's mind: (1) the actual inheritance and (2) God's blessing extended to non-Jews.

The Actual Inheritance

3. Have you ever wondered what your eternal inheritance will be? Look up the following verses and record elements of your inheritance.

Matthew 19:29 ______________________________

John 14:3 ______________________________

1 Corinthians 3:14 ______________________________

Revelation 21:1–7 ______________________________

Revelation 21:10–11, 18 ______________________________

Revelation 21:22–23, 27 ______________________________

Revelation 22:1 ______________________________

Revelation 22:2 ______________________________

Revelation 22:3–4 ______________________________

Revelation 22:5 ______________________________

Revelation 22:14 ______________________________

We who are in Christ are going to inherit more than we can imagine!

4. Do we have to go to heaven before we receive all of our inheritance? What inheritance in the Light do you already have?

Ephesians 1:13–14 ____________________

As believers, we've already received the Holy Spirit. He is the rock-solid pledge of our inheritance; a deposit of heaven. *Pledge* in this passage means "deposit" or "down payment." I pray your heart is enthralled with the Father's gift to you of His Holy Spirit.

Perhaps if we're basket cases, it's because we ignore our heavenly Father's gift of the Holy Spirit to us.

God's Blessing Extended to Non-Jews

The second thought Paul conveys is that God's blessings are extended to non-Jews.

5. What do the following Scriptures teach you in this regard?

Romans 10:12 ____________________

Romans 10:13 ____________________

At the heart of Paul's prayer is the message that God qualified any who call on the name of the Lord Jesus to be saved. What an extraordinary focus we can maintain in the midst of basket-case moments. This life is not all there is. Heaven awaits us. In addition, we praise God for the early inheritance He's given us—the Holy Spirit!

What's in Your Basket?

Basket Case

- Unqualified for heaven
- Working for earthly, not heavenly rewards
- Not filled with the Holy Spirit
- Not mindful of my salvation and inheritance in Christ

Extraordinary Life

- Qualified to share in the inheritance of the saints in light
- Working for heavenly rewards
- Filled with the Holy Spirit
- Mindful of my salvation and inheritance in Christ

♦ *Perhaps I'm a basket case because I forget about the wonderful gift of my inheritance in Christ. Perhaps I get too caught up in the passing details of the world.*

♦ *Perhaps I'm a basket case because I ignore the Father's gift of the Holy Spirit.*

♦ *Perhaps I'm a basket case because I'm not sure I'm qualified for heaven.*

Thinking It Over

♥ 1. Thank God for the glorious inheritance He's prepared for you in heaven.

♥ 2. Ask God to fill you with His precious Holy Spirit so you honor Him in all you do and say.

♥ 3. If you're unsure you're qualified for heaven, ask God to forgive you of your sins. Confess Jesus as your Lord and Savior. Commit your life to Christ and to serving Him.

Day 2: *Rescued from the Domain of Darkness!*

Father, Your love and power amaze me! My heart overflows with joy when I think of all You've done for me. Thank You for Your gracious, abounding love! Thank You for rescuing me from the domain of darkness. In Jesus's name. Amen.

◆ ◆ ◆

Mary pondered Paul's words long after she left church. The fact that she was qualified to share in the inheritance of the saints enthralled her. Since her family scraped together a living day to day, she could barely grasp the reality of her inheritance of the Holy Spirit and heaven.

◆ ◆ ◆

Paul woke wrestling with the memories of when he had persecuted Christians. Like an unwelcome guest, something often triggered the guilt and weighed down his heart like a heavy stone. Although such memories could have lured Paul into a black hole of despair, Paul chose instead to focus on Christ's forgiveness. Paul knew the darkness of the enemy, and he praised the God of Light!

◆ ◆ ◆

God Rescued Us from the Domain of Darkness

Reread Colossians 1:13.

1. From what has God rescued us? ____________________

These verses are powerful statements of God's glorious actions on our behalf and are worth memorizing.

Domain

In this passage the word *domain* means "power of rule" or "power of authority."

2. In verses 12–13 we see a contrast between two domains or powers of rule. What are they? ____

____

The kingdom of Satan has warred against the kingdom of God over mankind since the Garden of Eden (Genesis 2:16–17; 3:1–4). How does it make you feel to know you're not only the object of God's desire, but also of Satan's desire?

God's heart is for us to experience abundant life. Satan's plan is to steal, kill, and destroy (John 10:10).

Christ's domain is light. Satan's domain is darkness. You can't find a greater contrast.

3. Read the following and record God's role in regard to darkness.

Genesis 1:2–5 ____

John 1:1–5, 9–12 ____

God dispels darkness in creation and our soul! "As many as received Him" is the good news that even as the Spirit hovered over the darkness of the deep and brought light and life to earth, so the Spirit hovers over man's dark heart to bring the light and life of Christ to all who receive Him. Never stop praying that your children, family, and world will respond to Christ's Light.

4. How does Matthew 4:16 describe people before Christ's coming to earth?

____

5. What is Jesus's answer to the darkness? (Matthew 4:16–17) ________________________

____

6. Who did Jesus battle at the beginning of His ministry, before preaching, "Repent, for the kingdom of heaven is at hand"? Matthew 4:1–10 details that He battled
   ❑ His hometown synagogue ❑ The Pharisees ❑ ________________

7. Whose kingdom did Jesus battle throughout His ministry, yet prove Himself powerful over? Matthew 12:25–30 answers: ______________________________

____

8. Who fought Jesus every step of the way, even in his final days and hours?

   John 13:21, 26–27 shows us: ______________________________

9. How easy was it for Jesus to rescue us from the domain of darkness? Describe His Spirit according to the following verses:

   John 13:21 ______________________________

   Matthew 26:37 ______________________________

   Luke 22:44 ______________________________

10. What heavenly resource could Jesus have called on to avoid suffering on the Cross, though He didn't so that He could rescue us from Satan's domain? ____________

11. Bonus Question. How is Satan and his domain characterized? (See Matthew 4:3; Luke 22:53; John 8:44; 17:15; 2 Corinthians 4:4; 11:14; Ephesians 6:12; 1 Peter 5:8; Revelation 9:10–11; 12:9–10.) This is the one from whom God has rescued us.

Satan	His Domain
____________________	____________________
____________________	____________________
____________________	____________________
____________________	____________________
____________________	____________________
____________________	____________________
____________________	____________________

12. Why did the Son of God come into the world? Rewrite Acts 26:18 in the first person, replacing *their* and *they* with *my* and *I*.

____

____

Like a bright morning star (Revelation 22:16), Jesus came from heaven to earth to call us to Himself, the one true Light. We're invited to share in the inheritance of the saints in Light.

God Rescued Us

Rescue has two meanings: "to draw to one's self" and "to deliver."

Draw to One's Self

First, *rescue* carries an overtone: to draw to one's self. Using the illustration of a fireman, we can picture a rescue scene. A fireman rushes into a blazing house and calls a child's name. "Amber! Amber!" The fireman, seeing the child, swoops her into his arms.

God's heart is to draw us to Himself rather than let Satan's dominion have power over us (Luke 19:10). I pray your heart joins mine in singing "O Worship the King!"

Deliver

The second (and more normal) meaning of rescue is "to deliver." Jesus came from heaven to free us from Satan's dominion and deliver us to God's kingdom (John 6:38).

Continuing with our fireman illustration, we know a fireman doesn't stand in a burning house once he's drawn a child into his arms. Instead, he runs out of the house and takes the child to a place of safety. Likewise, our Lord not only rescues us from hell, but also delivers us to a place of glorious safety, His kingdom.

13. What evidence of evil, darkness, and perversion is there in our world today?

___

___

Whatever your thoughts, we clearly see evidence of Satan's influence.

14. List characteristics of Satan's demonic influence according to Luke 8:26–30 and Mark 5:1–5. ___

___

___

Can you imagine living for eternity under Satan's domain of darkness?

15. In Jesus, we see His and our Father's hearts. What did Jesus do for the demon-possessed man?

    ❑ Left him. ❑ Rescued him.

We can almost hear the conversation between the Father and Son as they looked on Satan's evil, dark domain on earth and planned our rescue. Their plan? For Jesus to infiltrate mankind. The Son of God became Son of man and broke the curse of sin and death.

Under whose domain do you want to live? Satan's or Jesus's? If you've never accepted Christ as Savior, call on Him today. He stands ready to rescue and deliver you so you can experience freedom from the domain of darkness, and have joy in the light of His presence.

What's in Your Basket?

Basket Case

- Troubled in spirit. Don't battle darkness with prayer and Scripture
- Forget to stand against the darkness from which God delivered me
- Ignore Jesus's warnings about Satan and demons

Extraordinary Life

- Rejoicing that God drew me to Himself in love
- Using prayer and Scripture to stand against Satan's darkness, despair, and temptations
- Praying for others to turn from the darkness and open their hearts to Christ

♦ *Perhaps I'm a basket case because I don't meditate on what God's done for me. I don't express my appreciation by closely following His ways.*

♦ *Perhaps I'm a basket case because I forget God desires to be close to me. I give Him little time.*

♦ *Perhaps I'm a basket case because I live like a captive of the darkness rather than a child of light.*

♦ *Perhaps I'm a basket case because although I'm saved, I ignore the reality of Satan or forget his ploys. I don't always pray and use Scripture to stand against the enemy.*

Thinking It Over

♥ 1. Express your gratitude to God the Father and Jesus for all they've done to rescue you from Satan's dominion. ______________________________

____

____

♥ 2. What personal sin, attitude, or habit might Satan use to keep you from experiencing God's best and fulfilling your kingdom duties? ______________________________

____

____

♥ 3. Pray about all that's on your heart. Remember... God the Father and Jesus love you so very much.

Day 3: *God Transferred Me*

Father, I praise You for reminding me of all You did for me when Christ rescued me from the domain of darkness. Thank You for giving Your beloved Son so I might be saved. Thank You for transferring me to His kingdom. In Jesus's name. Amen.

Mary's heart soared in praise as she listened to Paul's letter. Hearing about Satan's domain of darkness scared her, but also increased her love for the Lord Jesus.

◆ ◆ ◆

Paul rejoiced that he could write believers and explain how God rescued them from the domain of darkness. Although he realized Satan wasn't a popular topic of discussion, he knew it was important for believers to be aware of Satan so they could stand against him. Turning to the topic of God's empowerment and gifts—God's welcome package for Christians—Paul excitedly continued his letter.

◆ ◆ ◆

Today we're blessed by Paul's additional insights. READ COLOSSIANS 1:13–14, powerful verses.

1. We've already studied how God rescued us from the domain of darkness. In addition to rescuing, what else did God do? (v. 13) ______________________________

____

As you recall, *rescue* has two meanings: (1) "to draw to one's self" and (2) "to deliver." God not only delivered us from Satan's domain, He also transferred us to the kingdom of His beloved Son.

TRANSFERRED

Transfer means "to remove from one place to another." Many of us are familiar with business transfers. Sometimes people are transferred from one city or state to another, or from one position to another. *Transfer* had a special meaning in the ancient world. Often, when empires defeated nations, they deported the conquered people to the victor's land. Numerous examples exist in the Bible: Assyria deported some from the defeated Northern Kingdom. Babylon deported the Southern Kingdom. Closer to the Colossians' hearts would have been when Antiochus the Great transported 2,000 Jews from Babylonia to Colossae.

In today's verses, Paul explains our conquering King moved, or deported, us from the domain of darkness to the kingdom of His beloved Son.

2. Look up the following Scriptures. Record how God transfers us in a distinctively different way than earthly conquerors transfer captives.

   a) Earthly captors bound their captives and transported them in chains. Jesus ______________________________ those held captive by death (John 11:44).

   b) Earthly captors transported defeated people. Jesus transfers those who are ______________________________ through Himself (1 Corinthians 15:57).

c) Earthly captors forced captives to labor under heavy burdens. Jesus's yoke is ________________ and His burden ________________ (Matthew 11:30).

d) Earthly captors often stripped captives. Those in Jesus's kingdom receive ________________ (Revelation 3:5).

e) Earthly captors often shamefully marked or branded captives. Jesus marks those transferred to His kingdom with His ________________ (Ephesians 1:13).

What a glorious captor we have!

3. Bonus Question. We've already studied the terribleness of Satan's domain of darkness. What is Christ's kingdom like? Place the correct letter with the correct Scripture reference.
   a) It's promised to those who love Jesus.
   b) It's not of this world or realm.
   c) It's filled with those who have been born again.
   d) It's power and glory forever.
   e) It's healing.
   f) It's righteousness, peace, and joy in the Holy Spirit.
   g) It can't be shaken.

____ Romans 14:17 ____ Matthew 4:23 ____ Matthew 6:13 ____ John 3:3

____ John 18:36 ____ Hebrews 12:28 ____ James 2:5

God didn't rescue us so we would live aimless, defeated lives. We aren't as some Civil War slaves who, once freed, wandered, homeless, without meaningful work. We aren't as some prisoners, who, once released, find themselves without hope and without a home to which they can go. On the contrary, Ephesians 4:7–8 explains that Christ, victorious over the grave, ascended on high and led captive a host of captives. We are victorious, saved, former captives!

____

____

4. What else does Ephesians 4:8 explain that the Lord did? ________________

5. Ephesians 4:11, Romans 12:6–8, and 1 Corinthians 12:4–11 describe Christ's gifts to believers. List them in the space below. ________________

____

____

6. What is our kingdom title, according to 2 Corinthians 5:20? ______________

7. What is to be our response to being part of the eternal, glorious kingdom of God? Fill in the blanks using the following Scriptures.

   We are to show ______________ by offering to God ______________ service with ______________ (Hebrews 12:28)

8. What ministry has God given Christians, His ambassadors? ______________ (2 Corinthians 5:18–19)

God has assigned us to be His ambassadors and has given us the ministry of reconciliation.

9. What is the message we're to proclaim? ______________ (1 Peter 2:9)

He's given us the message! We have a job assignment from God! He did the work of saving us. Now, we have the assignment to tell others. It's our awesome privilege and God-given responsibility to live, not for ourselves, but rather to proclaim to others the excellencies of God's saving power and eternal forgiveness.

10. Each of us may wonder, *By what authority and power do I accomplish my kingdom assignment?* The following Scriptures answer that question.

    John 16:24 ______________

    Acts 1:8 ______________

How are we to perform our role as God's ambassadors? What if it's not natural for us to talk about spiritual issues with others? We ask God to excite and empower us to speak of Him.

11. What warning with a promise does Jesus give to those who have been transferred to His kingdom?
    Matthew 24:11–14 ______________

Paul recognized the privilege of being transferred to God's kingdom and serving God as His ambassador on earth. Do we?

Read Colossians 1:24–29.

12. How did Paul respond to God, who transferred him to the kingdom of His beloved Son? (Colossians 1:29) ______________

13. Did being transferred to God's kingdom mean Paul's work was all fun and smooth sailing? How did Paul describe his experience? (Colossians 1:24)
    ❑ As a party ❑ As suffering, but rejoicing in his suffering

14. For whose sake did Paul suffer? (Colossians 1:24) ______________________

15. Was Paul halfhearted about his kingdom assignment? If not, how does he describe his commitment to God? ______________________ (Colossians 1:25)

16. What did Paul fully carry out? ______________________ (Colossians 1:25)

What about us? Is it obvious to the world we're kingdom transferees? To what degree do we show gratitude to God by offering acceptable service with reverence and awe?

◆ ◆ ◆

> Mary pondered Paul's words. God had done so much for her. He rescued her from darkness. He transferred her to the kingdom of His beloved Son. He gave her a spiritual gift she wasn't using. He assigned her a kingdom title: Ambassador/Minister of Reconciliation. Now she pondered, *What am I doing for Christ?*

◆ ◆ ◆

I pray that we're pondering the same thing. God hasn't called us to read His Word and remain unchanged. As the time nears for Christ's reappearing, it's more important than ever for us to understand and fulfill our kingdom calling. God wants to use us to have an impact on our generation for Christ in our homes, churches, and world.

What's in Your Basket?

Basket Case

- Halfhearted ambassador for Christ
- Inactive minister of reconciliation
- Using my natural, human gift, but not kingdom gift
- Begrudgingly serving the Lord
- Refusing to suffer for Christ
- Prioritizing around worldly activities

Extraordinary Life

- Fully carrying out my role as an ambassador for Christ
- Active minister of reconciliation
- Using my kingdom gift
- Serving with gratitude, awe, and reverence
- Rejoicing in suffering
- Prioritizing around kingdom

◆ *Perhaps I'm a basket case because I'm more self-serving than God-serving.*

◆ *Perhaps I'm a basket case because I attempt to live for Christ in my own strength rather than allowing His power to flow through me.*

- *Perhaps I'm a basket case because I allow Satan to rob me of joy. I don't rejoice in the midst of serving Christ.*

Could it be we've been delivered from the domain of darkness and transferred to the kingdom of God's beloved Son, yet we allow Satan to rob us of joyful kingdom service? For example:

- We allow our children's sports and school activities to rob us of time with God.
- We allow the same activities to rob our children of sleep. Then, we let them sleep on Sundays rather than go to church. Thus, our children are robbed of God's Word and the church is robbed of our children.
- We let social and work commitments rob us of our time, gifts, and energy so we have little, if any, to give to Christ's kingdom.
- We neglect to raise our shield of faith when the enemy fires his flaming arrows at us. We're bound in doubt and despair although Christ has freed us to walk in newness of life.

Thinking It Over

♥ 1. Why not spend time talking to God about your priorities and what binds you or ties you in knots?

♥ 2. Jesus didn't withdraw from the world or spend His life as a monk. However, He did withdraw from social settings at times to pray. In prayer, He made decisions, such as which disciples to select. In prayer, He fought spiritual, physical, and emotional battles against Satan. Ask God how you could spend more purposeful time in prayer. Open your calendar before Him. Prioritize your activities around God's priorities for you and your family.

___

___

___

♥ 3. Prayerfully look over the lists of gifts God gives Christians. Which has He given to you?

___

___

♥ 4. Ask God to show you how you can use your gift(s) in the church. You may want to talk to your pastor or leaders for suggestions about how you can best serve the church.

___

___

♥ 5. Thank and praise God for transferring you to the kingdom of His beloved Son. Confess any sin. Experience His love and forgiveness as you recommit to being His ambassador.

Day 4: *God Redeemed and Forgave Me*

Father, as I begin my study today, I am overwhelmed with all You're teaching me. I'm both grateful and in awe of Your love. Please help me be Your faithful ambassador. In Jesus's name. Amen.

♦ ♦ ♦

Mary skipped along the street. She knew she was too old to skip, but she felt so lighthearted that she skipped anyway. *Who cares if someone sees me*, she assured herself. Paul's words echoed in her mind. She'd been transferred to the kingdom of God's beloved Son. Jesus entrusted her to be His ambassador! She was forever His.

♦ ♦ ♦

As Epaphras and Paul talked, they discussed the false teachers in Colossae. The ones who didn't deny Jesus but dethroned Him were a consistent threat to Christianity. They dethroned Jesus by denying He was equal to God. They dethroned the Lord Jesus by insisting He was one of many ways to God, not *the* Savior of the world.

♦ ♦ ♦

"Perhaps this is the worst enemy," Paul explained, "not denying the Lord Jesus outright, but dethroning Him; giving Jesus a prominent place, but not preeminence." Kneeling, Paul, Timothy, and Epaphras prayed in the preeminent name of the Lord Jesus.

♦ ♦ ♦

Is there a danger in our world of giving Jesus a prominent place, but not preeminence? Absolutely! The message of the Bible is that sin must be atoned for. Jesus is God, the Savior of the world. He is to be preeminent in our lives. The threat in Colossae and today is not being convinced Jesus is God, His Words are true, and He is the only one who can atone for sin and reconcile us to God.

The threat that the Colossians faced is the threat we face: give Jesus a prominent place in history, but don't acknowledge He's the only way to heaven. We must ask ourselves, however, if faith in Jesus for the forgiveness of sins is not the only way to God, why did God send Him to die for our sins? If any religion is fine, why did Jesus overturn the tables in the Temple and call the religious leaders white-washed tombs and their father the devil?

Bottom line, if Jesus is Lord, then He's not a liar or a lunatic, as some insinuate. Jesus's words are true. He came from heaven as He said He did, to save *the* world, not *one segment of* the world. As believers, we're to be "ready to make a defense" to everyone who asks about our faith in Jesus. We're to do so with conviction, yet with gentleness and reverence (1 Peter 3:15).

This week, we've studied what our heavenly Father did for us. Today, we begin an in-depth look at Jesus, focusing primarily on Colossians 1:14.

REREAD THE VERSE IN CONTEXT WITH VERSES 12–14, THEN ANSWER THE FOLLOWING QUESTIONS.

JESUS, GOD'S BELOVED SON

1. Jesus is: Colossians 1:13 and John 3:16 (Check two.)
   - ❑ One of many of the same kinds of sons of God
   - ❑ God's beloved Son
   - ❑ God's only begotten Son

2. Paul calls Jesus God's beloved Son because... Record Matthew 3:17.

____

____

3. Jesus accomplished the following on our behalf, which no one else can do (Colossians 1:14). ____

____

____

JESUS, OUR REDEEMER

Redemption means "liberation procured by the payment of a ransom." It's a combination of two words that, together, mean "the price for redeeming to liberate many from misery and the penalty of sins."

> A story told by Paul Lee Tan illustrates the meaning of redemption. He said that when A. J. Gordon was pastor of a church in Boston, he met a young boy in front of the sanctuary carrying a rusty cage in which several birds fluttered nervously. Gordon inquired, "Son, where did you get those birds?" The boy replied, "I trapped them out in the field." "What are you going to do with them?" "I'm going to play with them, and then I guess I'll just feed them to an old cat we have at home." When Gordon offered to buy them, the lad exclaimed, "Mister, you don't want them, they're just little old wild birds and can't sing very well." Gordon replied, "I'll give you $2 for the cage and the birds." "Okay, it's a deal, but you're making a bad bargain." The exchange was made and the boy went away whistling, happy with his shiny coins. Gordon walked around to the back of the church property, opened the door of the small wire coop, and let the

struggling creatures soar into the blue. The next Sunday he took the empty cage into the pulpit and used it to illustrate his sermon about Christ's coming to seek and to save the lost—paying for them with His own precious blood. "That boy told me the birds were not songsters," said Gordon, "but when I released them and they winged their way heavenward, it seemed to me they were singing, 'Redeemed, redeemed, redeemed!"

You and I have been held captive to sin, but Christ has purchased our pardon and set us at liberty. When a person has this life-changing experience, he will want to sing, "Redeemed, redeemed, redeemed!' "

—*Our Daily Bread*

The unsaved person's life is far worse than that of a caged bird. Unredeemed man has an unclean conscience (Hebrews 9:14). Unredeemed man will stand before a holy God who has explained that, without the shedding of blood, there's no forgiveness of sins (Hebrews 9:22). Unredeemed man will one day experience the truth: it's appointed once to die and after that comes judgment. (Hebrews 9:27). Unredeemed human sins are not considered as petty to God, but rather as filthy rags (menstrual rags).

4. Look up the following Scriptures that give God's solution, purpose, and result in light of man's sin problem.

   God's Solution: Galatians 3:13 ______________________________

   God's Purpose: Galatians 4:4–5 ______________________________

   The Result: Galatians 4:7 ______________________________

5. With what were we redeemed? (1 Peter 1:18-19) ____________________

6. What did Christ's blood purchase for us? (Hebrews 9:15) ________________

Isn't it joyous to know that we have cleansed consciences before God? In the Old Testament, sin was symbolically "put away," or separated, from sinners by the priest laying his hands on a goat, symbolically transferring the sins of the nation onto the goat. The goat was then sent into the wilderness. Because the goat carried away the sin which had been symbolically laid on it, they were no longer counted as guilty. Thus, the goat became the "scapegoat." In an ultimate act of grace, Jesus became our scapegoat. Every sin we've committed was laid on Him on the Cross.

Forgiveness of Sins

Forgiveness means "release from bondage or imprisonment, pardon for sins." What a beautiful word. Would you say the definition aloud and personalize it? "I'm released from the bondage and imprisonment of my sins. I'm pardoned. Totally."

Are we getting the picture of what Jesus did for us? Are we gaining a better understanding of why we should run as fast as possible from following a psychic or New Age guide? No one but Jesus could be a pure sacrifice to atone for our sins. No other name under heaven can forgive sin. It had to be Jesus or no one. Had Jesus not gone to the Cross, we would be held in Satan's power for eternity. We'd forever be slaves of sin. We'd forever be under the curse of sin and death.

Only God, who set the moral law, can forgive our sins against Him. "To the extent you did it to one of these brothers of Mine, even the least of them, you did it to Me" (Matthew 25:40). What were the sins in this passage to which Jesus was referring? Murder? No. Rape? No. The sin was: not feeding the sick, not visiting the imprisoned, and not clothing the needy. What is Jesus's response to not loving our fellow man as He commands? (See Matthew 25:41.)

We do well to remember that before our salvation, we were under the sentence of death and hell. We've all committed sins against others and God. To us, our rudeness toward another person may not be a crime. God calls it pride. When we look down our nose at someone or withhold love, He says it's as if we're doing it to Him (Matthew 25:40–41; Acts 22:7).

7. Reread Colossians 1:14. Personalize the following blank with the word *I* rather than *we*. Meditate on this wonderful verse. Memorize it. Tuck it in your heart and stand firm on it.

   In Jesus ________________ have redemption, the forgiveness of sins.

What's in Your Basket?

Basket Case

- Forget I'm forgiven
- Not sure I'm forgiven
- Trying to earn God's favor and forgiveness by what I do

Extraordinary Life

- Reconciled to God through Jesus, my Redeemer
- Daily remember and thank Jesus I'm forgiven
- Not perfect, but practicing God's ways

- ♦ *Perhaps I'm a basket case because I forget I've been redeemed and forgiven through Jesus's precious blood.*
- ♦ *Perhaps I'm a basket case because I live in fear rather than freedom. I worry about my sin rather than confess it.*
- ♦ *Perhaps I'm a basket case because I let my past weigh me down rather than live in the blessed joy that Jesus loves me and has released me from the guilt of my sins.*

♦ *Perhaps I'm a basket case because I've never faced my sin and guilt. I've been afraid, so I've ignored talking to God about it. I'm still under the curse of the Law, always trying to be good. I've never seen Christ as my sin-Redeemer and received Him as Savior.*

Thinking It Over

♥ 1. If you have Colossians 1:13–14 memorized, write it in the space below. If not, reread it; then record it.

____

____

♥ 2. What does Colossians 1:14 mean to you personally?

____

____

♥ 3. What is your prayer to God on the basis of Colossians 1:14?

____

____

Day 5: *The Preeminent Christ*

Heavenly Father, how can I ever thank You enough for redeeming me from the curse of the Law? Jesus, You saved me by shedding Your precious blood. I'm humbled at Your footstool, Your servant forever. In Jesus's name. Amen.

♦ ♦ ♦

Mary went to the well early the next morning. She wanted time to think about all she was learning. The silence did her good. The pristine morning made her feel as though she were one with God, and in fact, she knew she was. By His grace, she was saved. Nothing could separate her from His love. Quietly, she set her pot down beside the well and knelt, bowing her head in humble reverence. Had she ever bowed her knee and shown gratitude to her Redeemer for saving and forgiving her? Had she ever offered her life back to God? Conviction pressed her heart as she realized she had never done so. With her face to the ground, she quietly prayed and offered not only her life, but also her body to God for His use. As the Holy Spirit filled her, she stayed quietly in God's presence. It was as if while the sun rose on the land, the Son rose in her heart and filled her with His Light. Standing, she stared at the chalk-encrusted hills gleaming in the sunlight. "If they are that beautiful, what will your glorious kingdom of light be like, Lord?"

♦ ♦ ♦

Paul couldn't wait to write all that was on his heart about the preeminent Lord! After his visitors left, he immediately sat down and began dictating more of his letter.

◆ ◆ ◆

Jesus, the Image of the Invisible God

Read Colossians 1:15, noting how Paul refutes the Gnostics' false teachings about Christ and creation.

The Gnostics believed:

- Jesus wasn't fully God.
- Jesus was in the same order as angels.
- God was spirit and altogether good.
- The earth and matter were evil.
- God, who was good, couldn't touch evil. He was therefore *not* the Creator.

When Paul says Jesus is the *image* of the invisible God, he uses a word which means "likeness." In reference to Christ, it points to "His divine nature and absolute moral excellence." It's the same concept used in Genesis, when God said, "Let Us make man in Our image, according to Our likeness."

There's a distinction between Jesus *being* the image of God and our *being made* in the image of God. In Jesus we see man as God created him before the Fall. But we also see more. Image can refer to a representation or manifestation. Jesus is more than a representation of God; He is the manifestation of God.

John tried to capture the essence of Jesus's image. To describe Jesus, John used words like *life* and *light* (John 1:4). He described Christ as "the Word made flesh" having God's grace and truth (John 1:14).

1. Record John's description of Jesus. (John 1:14)
   "We saw His ________________, ________________ as of the only begotten from the Father, full of ________________ and ________________."

Life, light, glory, grace, and truth: God.

Jesus, the Firstborn of All Creation

Read Colossians 1:15–19.

The word *firstborn* in verse 15 is a Greek word implying two things: "priority to all creation" and "sovereignty over all creation." When Paul stated that Jesus is the firstborn over all creation, he meant in no uncertain terms that Jesus is God and existed before angels were created.

Having established that Jesus existed before any created being, including angels, Paul continues to discuss Jesus's relationship to creation.

2. Does Paul say Jesus was created or the Creator? (Colossians 1:16) ____________

3. What does Paul explain Jesus created?

- ❑ Things in heaven, but not things on earth
- ❑ Things on earth, but not in heaven
- ❑ Things in heaven and on earth
- ❑ Invisible things, like love, but not the earth
- ❑ Visible things, like the earth, but not invisible things
- ❑ Visible and invisible things
- ❑ Thrones
- ❑ Dominions
- ❑ Rulers
- ❑ Authorities
- ❑ Most things
- ❑ All things

4. For whom have all things been created? (Colossians 1:16)

For Jesus. Let those words ring through our ears for eternity. You and I were created *for Jesus*. Let us lay aside false impressions of who we are or thoughts that our days are to revolve around us. Instead, let's remember why we exist.

5. In whom do all things hold together? (Colossians 1:17) ____________

____

Author and pastor Warren Wiersbe, in *The Bible Exposition Commentary*, tells the story of a guide who "took a group of people through an atomic laboratory.... The tourists studied models of molecules and were amazed to learn that matter is made up primarily of space.... One visitor asked, 'If this is the way matter works, what holds it all together?' For that, the guide had no answer."

Not only is Jesus the agent of creation and one for whom the world was created, He is also the one who holds it together. As Christ holds all things together, He can hold us together.

6. List additional points about Jesus. (Colossians 1:18–19) ____________

____

____

Jesus, the Head (Beginning) of the Body, the Church

Head here is a metaphor for anything "supreme, chief, prominent." Again, we see Jesus's preeminence and place of authority. The church is Jesus's creation, just as the world is. It is His thought. Jesus brought the church into existence. He is the source of the church's life. Today, many problems and divisions are arising in the church. Only when we recognize Jesus as the head of the church and His Word as the authority will we find unity and peace.

Jesus, the Firstborn from the Dead

Jesus is not only the firstborn of creation and head of the church, He is also the firstborn from the dead. When we read this passage, we can't help but think of Christ's empty tomb on resurrection morning. As Jesus rose from the grave, so will we. As He ascended to the Father, so will we. He went first. We will follow.

Jesus is distinct from other prophets and religious leaders. No other person has died; been buried; raised; proved His resurrection by letting people touch Him, eat with Him, and talk with Him, then visibly, bodily ascended into the clouds. Witnesses of these events went to their grave refusing to deny what their eyes saw and their ears heard. Many were tortured, but refused to recant. Jesus isn't in the company of dead prophets. He's alive!

In Jesus Dwells All the Fullness of God

Fullness is used again by Paul in the sense of "that which is (has been) filled, such as a ship inasmuch as it is filled (i.e., manned) with sailors, rowers, and soldiers; completeness; abundance."

> The Gnostics defined *fullness* or *filled* as "the sum total of all the divine powers and attributes." *Dwell,* means to "settle."

Paul argued Jesus wasn't one of many divine spiritual mediators. He stated in no uncertain terms Jesus has the distinct sum total of all God's divine powers and attributes.

7. What's your response to the biblical teaching that the world was created by Jesus, through Jesus, for Jesus, when many schools teach your children that Jesus had nothing to do with creation? ______________________________

8. Do you agree or disagree that Christ has the right to dictate laws that govern us?

____

9. If you agree, what are your feelings about violating the Ten Commandments, about unmarried couples sleeping together, rather than marrying; having sex outside of marriage; coveting other people's bodies or possessions; lying; stealing; taking God's name in vain; harboring anger toward others; or giving God second place in one's life?

____

____

Jesus Reconciles All Things to Himself

Read Colossians 1:20–22.

Having addressed Jesus's relationship to creation, the church, and God, Paul returns to the theme in Colossians 1:13–14. Having said, "This is why I'm thankful. God rescued me from the domain of darkness and transferred me to the kingdom of His beloved Son. Now, let me tell you about His Son;" Paul discusses the great theme of our redemption. Paul's teaching culminates with the proclamation that Jesus is God, and able to accomplish what no other person can do.

10. What was God pleased to do through Jesus? (Colossians 1:20) ____________

____

____

Reconcile means "to reconcile completely; to bring back a former state of harmony." Doesn't it thrill your heart to know you've been brought back to the former state of harmony God had with Adam and Eve before the Fall?

11. Through what means did Jesus reconcile the world to God in peace? (Colossians 1:20, 22) ____________

____

____

12. In what three ways does Paul describe us prior to our salvation? (Colossians 1:21)

    a) ____________________

    b) ____________________

    c) ____________________

13. Alienated, hostile in mind, engaged in evil deeds. Friends, apart from Christ, that's how we are. We may not see ourselves like that, but that's how God sees our unredeemed state. What is Jesus's purpose in reconciling us? (Colossians 1:22)

____

____

"Holy and blameless and beyond reproach." "Alienated and hostile in mind, engaged in evil deeds." Jesus is going to present you and me before God one day, as either blameless, beyond reproach, in the holy array of Christ's righteous robes (Revelation 7:9–10), or alienated, hostile in mind, engaged in evil deeds, in sins we've committed against Him and others (John 8:24). Every thought will be revealed. Every sin exposed (Psalm 90:8).

It shouldn't be a hard decision to repent and confess Jesus as Lord. That is, unless a person wishes to deny that Jesus is Lord and that what He says is true in John 11:25–26; 12:48; 14:6.

What's in Your Basket?

Basket Case

- View Jesus as one of many spiritual paths to God; give Jesus a prominent place, not preeminence
- Still alienated, hostile in mind, engaged in sin
- Try to hold my family, marriage, business together instead of rely on Christ

Extraordinary Life

- Give Jesus preeminence; mindful Jesus is the head of the church; worship Jesus as creator
- Reconciled through Jesus's body and blood
- Pray to Jesus who holds all things together

♦ *Perhaps I'm a basket case because I forget Jesus created me for Himself.*

♦ *Perhaps I'm a basket case because I give Jesus a prominent place in my life, but not preeminence.*

♦ *Perhaps I'm a basket case because I work hard to hold everything together rather than rest in Jesus who holds all things together.*

♦ *Perhaps I'm a basket case because I worry more about my hair than my holiness.*

♦ *Perhaps I'm a basket case because I'm still engaged in sins I should put aside.*

Thinking It Over

♥ 1. What's on your heart after studying how Jesus is preeminent creator and upholder of all things?

In relation to yourself? ______________________________

In relation to others? ______________________________

♥ 2. Confess any area where you've failed to give Jesus first place or preeminence in relation to your commitments, thought life, work, habits, hobbies, finances.

____

____

♥ 3. Ask Jesus what adjustments you need to make in order to give Him His rightful place. Ask Him if there's anything you need to do to better teach your children eternal truths. Ask God to help you be better equipped to answer people's questions regarding the world and religion. (Read a book on the Jews or Islam, or turn the television station from a sitcom to a Bible history channel. Listen to Christian radio along with secular radio so you can be both current and biblically informed.)

____

____

♥ 4. Spend time thanking Jesus for who He is. Verse by verse, praise Him for each point and attribute. ____

____

____

____

____

____

____

I pray you're filled to the brim and overflowing with all you're learning about God the Father, Jesus Christ, and your relationship to them.

Weekly Wrap-Up

Where Am I? With which basket-case point do I most relate?

___

___

___

Where Do I Want to Be? To which aspects of extraordinary living is God calling me?

___

___

___

How Will I Get There? What golden nugget and/or verse do I want to remember to help me better handle my basket-case moments and live an extraordinary life?

___

___

___

Thinking of Others: What from this week's study do I want to share with someone to encourage or warn them?

___

___

___

♦ WEEK 4 ♦

PITIFUL OR POWERFUL?

If you've ever felt a little down in the dumps or wished someone would show you a little pity and help you out, that someone is on the scene in today's study.

♦ ♦ ♦

Mary was amazed at God! The more she learned about Him, the more she used her time at the well to visit with her friend, who wasn't a Christian. Mary explained to her how our natural state of sin causes us to be alienated from God.

Mary wasn't sure that she was convincing Rachel of anything, but at least she tried to share about Jesus. Mary's father's words were reassuring, "The Holy Spirit is the One who works in people's hearts to convict them of sin. *Your* responsibility is to speak the truth in love."

Later, when Rachel invited Mary to attend another "gathering," to explore ways to attain godliness through spirit guides, Mary declined.

Mary was thrilled when Onesimus came by later in the day. She hurriedly asked him a question that had been on her mind. "Paul said in this letter to us that Jesus would present us holy and blameless and beyond reproach—assuming we continue in the faith. Does that mean I can lose my salvation? Does it mean Satan can snatch me out of God's kingdom and take my soul back to his domain of darkness?"

"No, dear Mary," Onesimus assured her. Jesus has *eternally* sealed believers with the Holy Spirit. Jesus said, *"I give eternal life to them, and they will never perish; and no one will snatch them out of My hand."* Onesimus went on to explain that Paul was saying believers prove their faith by their steadfastness.

Mary loved how Onesimus explained spiritual truths. With new resolve, she determined to understand God's teachings better so she could help others as Onesimus helped her.

♦ ♦ ♦

Paul prayerfully pondered his next words to the Colossians. Having explained how God rescued them from the domain of darkness, transferred them into the kingdom of His beloved Son, redeemed and forgave them, he now wondered, *Do they fully grasp the mystery of Christ in them?*

Day 1: *Christ's Power in You*

> Father, I'm so thrilled to start my study this week! There's so much to learn. Help me fall more in love with You every day as You open my eyes to my relationship with Christ. In Jesus's name. Amen.

Today we embark on a week's journey that's going to equip us to stand against false teaching. Personally, I've found our study of Colossians to be both thrilling and challenging. As I mentioned in our first week, there are many lessons for us to discover and apply. This week, we're studying what Paul refers to as the "meat" of the Word. Pray God will open your mind to comprehend the riches of His Word.

Nothing rouses one's emotions as much as when a loved one is in danger. Paul, knowing the threatening pervasiveness of Gnosticism, legalism, mysticism, and asceticism, warns believers about these false religious teachings.

Read Colossians 1:24–29.

Rejoice in Suffering?

1. How does Paul approach his service to God? (Colossians 1:24)
   ❑ Begrudgingly ❑ Rejoicing

2. We might wonder, *Is Paul crazy? He's imprisoned in a house! How can he rejoice?* Paul isn't delusional, however. How does he describe his condition?
   ❑ Suffering ❑ A spiritual retreat

Paul admits he's suffering. He's honest about his situation. However, he chooses to rejoice. When Paul says that he rejoices *in* his sufferings, he's saying he rejoices *in the midst of* his suffering, *not he rejoices that he is* suffering. From Paul we learn: rejoicing is a choice. We can choose to praise God for being a present help in our suffering or we can feel sorry for ourselves. We can choose to look heavenward, knowing God is on the throne or we can worry ourselves to death. Perhaps if I'm a basket case, it's because I don't practice rejoicing *in the midst of* my sufferings.

3. For whose sake did Paul suffer? ______________________________

Paul wasn't trying to make anyone feel badly. He simply stated the truth. Paul's persecutors imprisoned him because the Jerusalem Jews were infuriated when he explained that God extended salvation to Gentiles (Acts 22:21).

Paul's sufferings were extensive. If we ever feel sorry for ourselves, perhaps we should consider his experiences, as outlined in 2 Corinthians 11:23–28.

4. First Peter 4:15–16 addresses reasons people may suffer—which aren't noble—contrasted with Paul's suffering, which was for Christ. Record those reasons.

Have you ever suffered because of a wrong you did? When I've suffered because of wrongs I've done, I've found it painful, yet constructive. God lets us bear the consequences of our wrongs so we learn from them. Perhaps if I'm a basket case, it's because I'm not learning from the consequences of my wrongdoings.

If I'm suffering for serving God, yet feel like a basket case, perhaps it's because I fail to consider how God may want to use my suffering to help someone else. Paul rejoices in the midst of his suffering as He serves Christ.

The Church, Christ's Body

Reread Colossians 1:24.

5. What is Christ's body, to which Paul refers? ______________________

The word *church* refers to "a gathering of citizens called out from their homes into some public place." In the Christian sense, it's used for an assembly of Christians gathered for worship, and then of the entire mystical body of Christ. Let's never forget Christ considers the body of believers as *His* body.

Read Acts 9:4–6.

6. How did Jesus view Paul's persecution of believers in Acts 9:4–6?
   ❑ As Paul persecuting Him ❑ As Paul persecuting others

Paul made a U-turn after the Lord Jesus confronted him on the Damascus Road. If persecuting believers were, in effect, persecuting Jesus, he would no longer persecute believers. Instead, he would love the church and die for Christ and His body of believers.

What about you? What is your relationship to the church (Jesus)? Do you love other believers (Jesus)? Are you willing to suffer for other believers as Paul did, "filling up what is lacking in them"? If there's a need in the nursery, do you prayerfully serve Christ there? If the youth need money for a missions trip, do you contribute to "fill up what is lacking" in their budget? If your church is divided, do you strive to be a peacemaker?

Perhaps we're basket cases because we want church members to be "filled up" with godliness yet we've not recognized our own lack of spiritual maturity. Perhaps we're basket cases because we've not considered our attitudes and actions against others as being *against Jesus*.

Reread Colossians 1:25.

7. What was Paul's ministry in the church? (Colossians 1:25) ____________________

8. Did Paul stop preaching after he was arrested? ____________________

9. What is your God-given ministry in the church? ____________________

10. What gets in the way of you fulfilling your ministry? ____________________

When Paul says he "fills up what is lacking in Christ's afflictions," he's not referring to Christ's atoning (or saving) sufferings on the Cross. As Kenneth Wuest explains in *Wuest's Word Studies from the Greek New Testament for the English Reader*,

> "The afflictions of Christ" here do not refer to His expiatory sufferings on the Cross, but to His sufferings endured in His humiliation before that event; sufferings for righteousness' sake, sufferings incurred through exhausting service, heart-sufferings due to the opposition of sinners, sufferings that were the result of persecution... These sufferings incurred during His earthly ministry were necessarily curtailed by reason of His limited life on earth, and needed to be continued in His servants if the work of preaching the Word was to be carried on. Thus, all the saints down the ages are partakers of these sufferings when they are faithful to the obligation they have of preaching the Word.

God's Mystery Manifested

Read Colossians 1:25–27.

11. How did Paul describe the word he proclaimed? (v. 26) ____________________

When Paul referred to his message as a "mystery manifested," it was a direct confrontation to false teachers who wooed people from the simplicity of the gospel. False teachers urged people to add to their faith "fullness of knowledge." They claimed only a select few could experience fullness of knowledge, and it was only available through the mystical experience they offered.

12. Rather than God being secretive, what "mystery" does Paul say God willed to be known? (v. 27) ____________________

____

God willed to reveal the riches of His glory.

Christ in You, the Hope of Glory

What is the glorious mystery once hidden but now revealed? The mystery is the birth of the church. The mystery is God uniting Jews and Gentiles into one body in Christ (1 Corinthians 12:13; Galatians 3:27–28). However, there's more. Just as television commercials tell us what we get for a certain price and then say, "But there's more," so Paul explains there's even more: Christ is *in* the believer. Now that's a mystery!

13. What's the significance of Christ being "in" us? Fill in the following blanks using the correct word from this list: *mighty, complete, works, glory, power.*

    Christ is our hope of ____________________ . (Colossians 1:27)

    Every person can be presented ________________ in Christ. (Colossians 1:28)

    Christ's ____________________ is in us. (Colossians 1:29)

    Christ's power is ____________________ . (Colossians 1:29)

    Christ ____________________ within us. (Colossians 1:29)

Christ in you (Colossians 1:27). You in Christ (Colossians 1:28). What a glorious mystery revealed! What a glorious fulfillment of that for which Christ prayed (John 17:20–23).

To what degree do you appreciate the mystery of Christ in you? Paul isn't saying we're gods. He's explaining what Jesus taught before His death: all believers are given the Holy Spirit to accomplish God's work (John 14:16–20; 15:26; Acts 1:8). Meditate on these meaty teachings!

It's a mystery that Christ is in believers through the Holy Spirit (Romans 8:9–11). It is because of the fact that Christ is in us that we will one day be presented complete before God. Marvel in this mystery! Marvel in God's grace.

What's in Your Basket?

Basket Case

- Not in Christ; trying to get to heaven by being good
- Not serving Christ's body, the church
- Grumbling in the midst of suffering
- Suffering the consequences of wrong choices

Extraordinary Life

- In Christ, saved by grace, baptized, filled, empowered by the Holy Spirit
- Loving and serving Christ's body, the church
- Rejoicing in the midst of suffering
- Suffering for Christ

- *Perhaps I'm a basket case because I don't rejoice in the midst of my circumstances; I grumble.*
- *Perhaps I'm a basket case because when I'm suffering, I don't consider how God may one day use my suffering to help me comfort others.*
- *Perhaps I'm a basket case because I expect Christians to be "filled up" with all godliness; spiritually mature. I've not recognized that believers lack full spiritual maturity this side of heaven.*
- *Perhaps I'm a basket case because I've not recognized that my wrong attitudes, words, and actions toward others are toward Jesus.*
- *Perhaps I'm a basket case because I don't learn through the consequences of my wrongs that cause me to suffer.*
- *Perhaps I'm a basket case because I've not committed my life to serving God. I'm not continually filled with God's Spirit as Ephesians 5:18 commands.*
- *Perhaps I'm a basket case because I serve God in my own futility and bear little fruit. I need to yearn to experience Christ's Spirit working mightily in me.*

Thinking It Over

♥ 1. How is God speaking to you about Christ being in you? ____________________

____

____

♥ 2. How is God speaking to you about your relationship to other believers and the church? ____

____

____

♥ 3. What is significant to you about rejoicing in suffering? ____________________

____

____

♥ 4. With which basket-case scenario do you most relate? Use this time to prayerfully let God grow and mature you. He wants to use you for His kingdom.

____

____

DAY 2: *Your Potential in Christ*

Lord, as I study today open my eyes to Your desire for me. Help me to see my potential because Christ is in me. Grow me, Lord, so I can live an extraordinary life for You. In Jesus's name. Amen.

♦ ♦ ♦

Paul's heart was on fire for Christ. Since seeing and hearing the ascended Lord on the Damascus Road, he was dramatically changed. Marveling that God set him apart while in his mother's womb to serve Christ, Paul bowed his knees in praise. Little did Paul realize that his childhood aspiration to be a Pharisee would prepare him to be a strategic author of the New Testament.

◆ ◆ ◆

Mary's mind overflowed with all she was learning. Though she entered salvation by simple faith, she was now discovering the deep and glorious riches of her spiritual inheritance in Christ. Mary realized she didn't need "fullness" *apart* from Christ. Rather, her needs and desires could be met only *in* Christ. Mary committed to spend the rest of her life learning about Christ.

◆ ◆ ◆

READ COLOSSIANS 1:28 TO 2:1.

We've been challenged by how Paul rejoiced in his suffering. Today we're challenged by Paul's love for Christ and believers.

1. What or whom does Paul proclaim, preach, herald, announce? (v. 28) ____________

____

2. In addition to proclaiming Jesus, what did Paul do? Check two.
   ❑ Pitied himself ❑ Admonished ❑ Taught

Admonish means "to warn and exhort." *Teach* means "to impart instruction, instill doctrine, explain and expound." Good teachers, preachers, and parents both warn and instruct.

3. Record words that describe the intensity with which Paul proclaimed Jesus, admonished, and taught. (Colossians 1:29; 2:1) ____________

____

____

Paul *labored*, from a word that means "grew weary, tired, exhausted." Paul *strived*, from the original word that means he "contended with adversaries and endeavored with strenuous zeal." Paul engaged in a *struggle*, denoting "a contest, battle, action at law, trial."

4. Paul labored, strived, and struggled on behalf of not just the Colossian believers, but for whom else? (Colossians 2:1) ____________

Sisters, we're among those for whom Paul struggled. We've not yet met Paul, but we will one day. After bowing before our Lord, I imagine that he'll be among those whom we thank.

5. According to whose power did Paul labor and strive? ____

Paul said Christ's power mightily worked within him. *Working* means "working, efficiency, used only of superhuman power, whether of God or the devil." It is power in exercise. Our word *energy* is derived from this word. *Mightily* is power in the sense of natural inherent ability. *Wuest's Word Studies from the Greek New Testament for the English Reader* says, "The struggle is carried on in proportion, not to his natural powers, but to the mightily working energy of Christ within him."

Isn't this exciting? The mighty working energy of Christ is in you if you're a Christian. This is a mystery we shouldn't forget. This is why we hope not just for heaven, but also for what Christ can do in and through us today!

For what reason did Paul labor to the point of exhaustion, battle against Satan, warn us of false teachings, and equip us with the truth? The answer is found in the following verses. It's Paul's passion (Christ's passion in him), for believers to mature in their faith.

Perhaps if I'm a basket case, it's because I try to serve God in my power. Instead, I need to open my heart and mind to Christ's mighty working power within me.

Read Colossians 2:2–10.

6. List evidences of Christians who are maturing in their faith.

   a) Hearts are ________________, having been knit together in ________________. (Colossians 2:2)

   b) Believers attain to all the ________________________ that comes from the full assurance of understanding. (Colossians 2:2)

   c) Believers attain to a true knowledge of God's mystery, ________________. ________________________________ (Colossians 2:2)

   d) Believers understand that in Christ are ________________ all the treasures of wisdom and knowledge. (Colossians 2:3)

   e) Believers aren't ______________ with persuasive arguments. (Colossians 2:4)

   f) Believers are disciplined and __________________ in their faith. (Colossians 2:5)

   g) Believers ____________________ in the Lord. (Colossians 2:6)

   h) Believers are firmly __________________ and built up in Christ. (Colossians 2:7)

   i) Believers are ______________ in their faith and overflow with ______________. (Colossians 2:7)

Christ's Potential for You

Christ mightily, energetically works within Paul, giving him words and insight by which to help us mature in our faith. Consider the above points and your degree of Christian maturity.

7. In which of the above areas do you need prayer? ______________________________

___

An Encouraged Heart

Reread Colossians 2:1–2.

Heart here means "the center and seat of spiritual life; the soul or mind; the fountain and seat of thoughts, passions, desires, appetites, affections, purposes, endeavors." Paul knows the effects of a discouraged heart. Therefore he labors so that they may possess an encouraged heart.

8. What happens when you're discouraged? How does discouragement affect your energy, attitudes, relationships, and even zeal for God? ______________________________

___

Just as our core body strength affects the rest of our body, so our core spiritual strength affects our thoughts, emotions, and endeavors. The Lord doesn't want you to have a discouraged (depressed) heart. Rather, He wants to encourage you. *Encouragement* here means "to call to one's side, to speak in order to give instruction, admonish, exhort, console, strengthen by consolation, comfort."

9. In what way has Jesus established a means by which to call you to His side, give you instruction, warn you, strengthen you by consoling you, and comfort you? (John 14:16–17) ______________________________

___

When discouraged or depressed, we can go to God. We can be still and worship Him as God (Psalm 4:3–4). We can pour out our heart to Him. We can ask Him to fill us with the Helper, the Holy Spirit. If our heart's desire is to serve and glorify God (James 4:3), He will speak to our heart and mind, instructing, strengthening, comforting, and warning us (Psalm 32:8).

Hearts Knit Together in Love

Reread Colossians 2:2.

I love this visual of believers' hearts knit together. Knit fabrics are a series of interlocking loops that result in flexible fabric. How important it is for believers to link together, yet remain flexible in God's hands.

10. Are you knit together in love with other believers? Are you flexible in God's hands and flexible with others to whom God has joined you? ______________________

____

Wealth and Hidden Treasures in Christ

Reread Colossians 2:2–3.

You may be thinking, *How much more could Jesus desire for us?* Yet, in Colossians 2:2, Paul speaks of Christ's energy mightily working in us in relation to wealth. *Wealth* here is "riches, fullness, and abundance." God wants us to attain a full, rich, abundant knowledge of Christ (John 10:10).

11. Why do Paul and Jesus want believers to obtain this fullness? (Colossians 2:3)

____

____

Are you a seeker of hidden treasures? *Hidden* means "secret, stored up." Treasures is the place in which good and precious things are collected and laid up. Paul wants us to understand good and precious things are laid up, hidden, and stored in Christ. Whereas false teachers woo seekers to "fullness" apart from Christ, Paul exhorts us to seek every good and precious thing in Christ.

Wuest notes,

> The force of this passage then is this: all, and not merely some of the treasures of wisdom and knowledge are contained in Christ; therefore the search for them outside of Him is doomed to failure. But not only are they in Christ, but they are contained in a hidden way. Therefore they do not lie on the surface, but must be sought for earnestly, as men seek for hidden treasure. They are not matters of external observances, such as the false teachers enjoined, but to be apprehended by deep and serious meditation.

12. Sisters, to what degree have you found there is more to Jesus and the Bible than first meets the eye? Share a treasure you've found in Christ. ______________________

____

____

Not Deluded

Reread Colossians 2:4.

Paul struggles for us so we're not deluded. *Delude* means "to reckon wrong, to deceive by false reasoning."

13. Is it possible for something to appear right, but be wrong? Who did Jesus confront about that very thing? (Matthew 23:27–28) ______________________________

____

____

Today, as in Paul's day, there's a danger of believers being deluded and misled. As a matter of fact, our so-called Christian nation is in danger. Consider this statistic from *The Barna Update*,

> Sixty-one percent of today's young adults had been churched at one point during their teen years but they are now spiritually disengaged (i.e., not actively attending church, reading the Bible, or praying).... For most adults, this pattern of disengagement is not merely a temporary phase in which they test the boundaries of independence, but is one that continues deeper into adulthood, with those in their thirties also less likely than older adults to be religiously active. Even the traditional impulse of parenthood—when people's desire to supply spiritual guidance for their children pulls them back to church—is weakening. The new research pointed out that just one-third of twentysomethings who are parents regularly take their children to church....
>
> Interestingly, here was one area in which the spiritual activities of twentysomethings outpaced their predecessors: visiting faith-related Web sites.
>
> —"Most Twentysomethings Put Christianity on the Shelf Following Spiritually Active Teen Years," The Barna Group, http://www.barna.org

Faith-related Web sites can be good if they proclaim Jesus as Savior and recognize the authority of the Bible. However, how will young adults discern if they're on biblically sound Web sites if they're not in God's Word? Colossians 2:5–7 answers: good discipline, stability of faith, walk in Christ, firmly rooted, built up in Christ, established in faith, overflow with gratitude.

If our generation isn't filled with Christ's Spirit, rooted in God's Word, established in our faith, and overflowing with gratitude to God, why wouldn't the next generation seek another religion to meet their needs?

What's in Your Basket?

Basket Case

- Discouraged
- Deluded
- Attaining worldly wealth and treasures
- Not discipled, walking in the flesh
- Striving in my own power for self-interests

Extraordinary Life

- Encouraged
- Heart knit in love with other believers
- Attaining wealth and treasure hidden in Christ
- Overflowing with gratitude
- Jesus's power and energy mightily working in me
- Striving to help others know Christ, the treasure

♦ *Perhaps I'm a basket case because I'm deluded with psychics, tarot cards, and reincarnation.*
♦ *Perhaps I'm a basket case because I don't seek treasures and wealth in Jesus.*
♦ *Perhaps I'm a basket case because when discouraged, I seek human counsel rather than the Helper's counsel.*
♦ *Perhaps I'm a basket case because my roots in Christ are shallow. I'm not rooted and built up in God.*
♦ *Perhaps I'm a basket case because I walk by my will and mind rather than Christ's.*
♦ *Perhaps I'm a basket case because I'm not close to other Christians. I'm not knitted to others in love.*

Thinking It Over

♥ 1. How is God speaking to you? With which basket-case scenario do you most relate? Pray about whatever is on your heart. ______________________________

____

____

♥ 2. How is God speaking to you about your heart being encouraged and knit together in love with others? ______________________________

____

____

♥ 3. For which blessings of knowing Christ and discovering hidden treasures of wisdom and knowledge in Him do you yearn? ______________________________

____

____

♥ 4. For whom are you concerned because they're unstable in their faith or deluded? How will you respond to God's call to strive, labor, and struggle for them?

Bless you as God uses you in our generation and the next!

Day 3: *Gnosticism*

Father, as I study Your Word, help me discover Your hidden treasures. Unearth all You have for me so I can serve Your kingdom. In Jesus's name. Amen.

◆ ◆ ◆

Paul realized his warnings about false teachers sounded redundant. However he was all too familiar with their tactics. First, false teachers cast an air of intellectual, spiritual snobbery, claiming superior power apart from Christ. Second, false teachers claimed Jesus emanated from God, but wasn't fully God. Some false teachers said Jesus wasn't fully man. They insisted He was a spirit who left no footprints. Aware of their teachings, Paul prayed that believers would denounce any teaching that denied Jesus was the Son of God, Son of man in whom salvation is complete.

◆ ◆ ◆

Mary was shocked to learn that a childhood friend attended angelic enlightenment sessions at Rachel's house and in addition had tried to contact her dead mother through a "spirit guide." As Mary listened to Paul's letter, she prayed, "Lord, let me hear something that will help me talk to her."

◆ ◆ ◆

Captive

The next three days are important. In them, you'll learn the five "isms" threatening Paul's day and ours: Gnosticism, syncretism, legalism, mysticism, and asceticism. Each ism incorporates the following tactics Satan has used since Eden:

1st — Satan poses as an angel of light. He offers "enlightened" teachings.
2nd — He places a lie alongside God's truth.
3rd — He uses the deluded to delude others. Eve is a perfect example of one who, having been deluded, then deludes Adam.

Read Colossians 2:8.

1. What was Paul's concern? That no one be taken:
   - ❑ For granted
   - ❑ For fools
   - ❑ Captive

Paul knew what it meant to be taken captive. He also understood there were different forms of captivity. One could be spiritually free but physically captive. Or, a person could be physically free yet spiritually captive. Jesus, who came to set captives free (Luke 4:18), mightily works through Paul to warn believers not to be taken captive.

2. List ways Paul says we can be taken captive. (Colossians 2:8) ________________

____

____

Philosophy and Empty Deception

Philosophy, in Greek, means "love of wisdom." Paul isn't speaking against all philosophy. He was a gifted philosopher! He was warning against Gnosticism. The brand of Gnosticism in Colossians contained several characteristics

- It was Jewish, stressing the need for observing Old Testament laws and ceremonies.
- It was philosophical, laying emphasis on some special or deeper knowledge.
- It involved the worship of angels as mediators to God.
- It was exclusive, stressing the special privilege and "perfection" of the select few who belonged to the philosophical elite.
- It was Christological, but denied the deity of Christ.
- It offered salvation from the oppressive bonds of material existence through gnosis, or "knowledge."

3. Although we might feel removed from issues early believers faced, the issues of Paul's day are the issues of our day. For instance, the following Gnostic classes are offered today. As you reread Colossians 2:8, review these class descriptions and underline true biblical concepts. Mark through false teaching.

Contacting Your Spirit Guides and Angels

Angels have been in every religion and culture as messengers, guardians, and God's protective army. It is simple to reach them; belief is the key. Learn their names and functions to help you to call upon the best helper for your specific goals.

Meditation Class

This class explains and defines meditation. The student will learn the steps of meditation to visualize for success, synergism, and manifesting desired abundance as well as receiving messages from spirit guides, angels, or deceased loved ones.

These classes are taught by a popular author and speaker! But the Bible teaches us angels are not to be worshipped or sought after. It teaches us to meditate on God and His Word. God forbids us to seek spiritists and mediums.

4. How could you use what you're learning to respond to someone involved in false teaching, such as the above modern Gnosticism classes? ________________

____

Read Colossians 2:9–10.

One Gnostic teaching is that Jesus is not fully God. A Gnostic claim of both the first century and today is Jesus is one of several manifestations or emanations from God.

5. How does Paul respond to Gnosticism and syncretism (fusion of differing systems of belief in philosophy or religion) which deny the deity of Jesus and argue that Jesus is a son of God as all of us are sons (or daughters) of God? (Colossians 2:9)

____

____

In Colossians 2:9, Paul explains "all the fullness of Deity" dwells in Jesus. According to *Wuest's Word Studies from the Greek New Testament for the English Reader*,

> Paul is declaring that...they were no mere rays of divine glory which gilded Him, lighting up His Person for a season and with splendor not His own; but He was, and is, absolute and perfect God.... Here the word "divinity" will not do; only the word "deity."... Modernism believes in His divinity, but in a way different from the scriptural conception of the term. Modernism has the pantheistic conception of the deity permeating all things and every man. Thus divinity...was resident in Christ as in all men. Paul never speaks of the divinity of Christ, only of His deity. Our Lord has divine attributes since He is deity, but that is quite another matter from the Modernistic conception.

6. What point did Paul clarify in Colossians 2:9 to refute the false teaching that Jesus didn't dwell in bodily form; that He was a spirit, who left no footprints; and that He couldn't be fully God and at the same dwell in bodily form? ____________________

____

Reread Colossians 2:10.

7. Write out Colossians 2:10 in the first person, meditating on the wonderful words that remind us:

- Christ is head over all.
- We don't need angelic intermediaries to reach Him.
- In Christ we're complete. In Christ we're whole.

____

____

____

What's in Your Basket?

Basket Case

- Philosophy of the world
- Easily deceived
- Captivated by human traditions
- Captivated by psychic readers, tarot cards, past lives, mediums
- Seek fullness apart from Christ

Extraordinary Life

- Wisdom of Christ
- Guard against deception
- Not captive to church tradition; open to Christ's Spirit
- Not captivated by false teachings
- Filled and complete in Christ

♦ *Perhaps I'm a basket case because I worry about my children and their future rather than prayerfully teach them God's Word so that they are committed to follow Christ.*

♦ *Perhaps I'm a basket case because I'm worried about false teachings and practices with which I once was involved. Rather, I should repent and accept Christ's grace and forgiveness.*

♦ *Perhaps I'm a basket case because I'm not convinced that Jesus is the unique Son of God in whom all the fullness of deity dwells; I think of Jesus as one of many ways to God.*

Thinking It Over

♥ 1. What has been most enlightening to you about Gnosticism in Paul's day and ours?

____

____

♥ 2. Are you as alarmed as Paul about Gnosticism? If so, what responsibility are you taking to guard against it? What might you warn friends of who attend Gnostic "personal development classes"? ______________________________

____

____

♥ 3. Glance over today's lesson. What stirs your heart the most? Why?______________

____

____

♥ 4. What might Jesus want you to do as a result of today's lesson? Be more faithful to pray for 20somethings and 30somethings or others? Teach a young adult or other class? Be more committed to God's Word? Take your children to church?

____

____

Sisters, I pray God's blessings on you as you grow in the knowledge of the Lord Jesus Christ.

Day 4: *Legalism*

Father, Your mercies are new every morning. You are with me through the day and when evening comes, You tuck me in bed. Thank You for the assurance I'm saved by Christ alone. In Jesus's name. Amen.

◆ ◆ ◆

The debate raged. A sect of Jews told Mary's father he needed to be circumcised. Hours of discussion followed. Mary heard her father and his friends weigh the pros and cons of the surgical procedure, including the cost, pain, recuperation period, and spiritual benefit. Mary's mother pleaded with her father, "If you want to be circumcised, go ahead. But please don't put our son through surgery just to please some religious people who insist on their ancient tradition." Nothing more was said about it. Then Onesimus mentioned that Paul addressed circumcision in his letter. That night, people walked a little faster to the church to hear Paul's insights on the subject.

◆ ◆ ◆

Paul sat at his table and rubbed his eyes. It had been a long day and he hadn't slept the night before. He was getting antsy, not used to being confined. How he longed to visit Colossae and share in person that salvation isn't gained by man's righteousness. Jesus bought our salvation with His blood.

◆ ◆ ◆

Circumcised Hearts

Yesterday we studied Gnosticism. Today Paul addresses another ism against which believers must guard: legalism. In Christian theology, *legalism* is a negative term used in reference to people who have an improper fixation on laws or codes of conduct. Without respect to God's grace, they insist everyone adhere to their code of conduct. They leave no room for God's grace or the Spirit to work in fresh ways.

Read Colossians 2:9–17.

1. In whom or what does Paul say believers are made complete, thereby requiring no other rite for salvation?
   ❑ Baptism ❑ Circumcision ❑ The Law ❑ Jesus

2. What title or position does Jesus occupy?
   ❑ Lower than angels ❑ Equal to the sons of God ❑ Head over all

3. Jesus is head over what? (Colossians 2:10) ______________________________

4. Why do you think Paul felt it important to explain Jesus is head over all as he addresses the subject of Jewish legalism with Gentile believers? ______________________________

____

5. What is the "hot" issue being addressed? (Colossians 2:11)
   - ❑ If the *hallel* had to be sung every Sunday or if a new song could be introduced
   - ❑ If instruments could be part of the worship service
   - ❑ If males need to be circumcised to be saved

Physical circumcision is the act of surgically removing a male's foreskin. God introduced circumcision to Abraham as a religious rite when Abraham was 99 years old.

6. READ GENESIS 17:10–12. What was circumcision a sign of? (v. 11) ____________

____

If you read Genesis 17:14, can you understand why these Jews became legalistic about circumcision?

7. What happened to the person who refused to be circumcised? ______________

____

I'm not sure if it was intended or not, but there is a play on words in Genesis 17:14. In effect, God says, "If you don't cut it off, I'm cutting you off!" That's pretty straightforward language. And it helps us see why some Jews insisted Gentile converts be circumcised.

Read Acts 15:1.

8. What did the Jewish legalists in Acts 15:1 teach? ______________________

Continue reading Acts 15 to find out what Paul, Barnabas, Peter, and James (Jesus's half brother) said. It was the first church council debate.

9. What was Peter's final statement in support of Paul and Barnabas? (Acts 15:7–11)

____

____

In Christ Alone

In Colossians 2:9–15, we continue to see the theme that our salvation, wisdom, knowledge, treasure, and fullness are in Christ alone (Colossians 1:2, 13–14, 22; 2:3, 5, 6, 7, 9, 10, 11).

10. In Colossians 2:11, we find another reference to what believers have in Christ. What is it? ____

____

Good news! "In Christ, God's Son, the Messiah, you, my Gentile friend, were circumcised." A simplified illustration, though inadequate, would be if you were going to a show with a friend, but didn't have a ticket. However, the person you were with was the owner of the theatre. As you walk through the door, the owner calls out, "She's with me." No further questions are asked. You don't have to purchase a ticket because you're with the owner.

"They're with Me," Jesus announces. "No piece of skin is going to keep a person out of heaven. I've checked their spirit all the way to heaven."

11. According to Colossians 2:11, is being circumcised important?
   ❑ Yes ❑ No

12. Is a believer's circumcision done with or without hands? ______________________

____

13. Who performs a believer's circumcision? (Colossians 2:11; Romans 2:29)

____

14. What does God the Holy Spirit circumcise? (Romans 2:29)
   ❑ The outer skin ❑ The heart

15. What does God remove from us? (Colossians 2:11) ______________________

____

Consider the following synopsis of Jewish versus believer's circumcision.

Jewish Circumcision
- Physical surgery
- A small part of the external body
- Done with human hands
- Had no power over sin

Believer's Circumcision
- Spiritual surgery
- The whole body of sin in the heart
- Done by the Spirit, without hands
- Results in available power over sin

The body of flesh is a reference to our sin nature. Consider how Wuest explains the removal of the body of flesh by the circumcision of Christ:

> The fleshly circumcision removed only a portion of the body. In spiritual circumcision, through Christ, the whole corrupt, carnal nature is put away like a garment which is taken off and laid aside. . . . Its power is broken, and it has no more power over the believer than he allows it to have.

Paul makes it clear: external circumcision doesn't save.

16. How are we saved? (Colossians 2:12) ______________________________

____

Repeatedly, we see that we're saved through faith in Christ's work at Calvary.

Baptized with Christ

At this point, Paul proceeds to talk about our death, burial, and resurrection in Christ, symbolized through water baptism.

At that time, water baptism was:
- ❑ For adults
- ❑ For the repentance of sin
- ❑ By immersion (A person was lowered into the water and then raised up out of the water.)

As with physical circumcision, physical baptism doesn't save. It's an external expression of an internal experience with Christ.

17. Explain how water immersion is an external symbol of the believer's internal identification in Christ's death, burial, and resurrection. (Colossians 2:12)

____

____

____

When we accept Christ's death as payment for our sins, our old nature is identified as crucified with Christ (Galatians 2:20). When a person is immersed in water, this symbolizes the old dead self being buried with Christ. When a believer is raised from the water, it symbolizes the person's identification with Jesus's resurrection to new life by the power of God.

As Jesus was raised, yet changed, so Christians are raised and spiritually changed. Christians are new creations (2 Corinthians 5:17) because God's Spirit resides in them. Christians are those who have experienced new birth (John 3:5–6).

How does Paul express our resurrection life in Colossians 2:13?
- ❑ Believers are made alive together with Christ.
- ❑ Believers must try in their own strength to keep the Old Testament Law.

This is why water baptism is special to believers. It's not salvation. It's our joyful announcement, "This is what I did... put my faith in Jesus! This is what He did... took my sins to the Cross and my sin nature to the grave! This is what Jesus gave me... His Holy Spirit by whom I can walk in newness of life."

18. Before your salvation, how does God view you and your spiritual condition? (Colossians 2:13) ____

____

Before salvation, we are dead in our sins and the "uncircumcision of our flesh." *Dead* is a metaphor for "spiritually dead, destitute of a life that recognizes and is devoted to God, given up to trespasses and sins, destitute of force or power, inactive, inoperative." Dead is our spiritual condition prior to salvation. The divine Spirit of God isn't operative in unsaved people who sin without remorse.

Spiritually dead doesn't mean spiritually annihilated. It means spiritually separated from God. Paul explains that prior to salvation we're dead *in* our transgressions. *Transgressions* carries overtones of "falling beside or near something, a lapse or deviation from truth and uprightness, a sin, misdeed." Were we to die in this fallen state, we'd be separated from God; fallen eternally in the kingdom of darkness.

19. However, through Christ, what does God do? (Colossians 2:13) ______________

____

Instead of abandoning us while we were dead in our sins, God forgave our sins and made us alive together with Christ! If you've not said, "Hallelujah," and responded to His offer of salvation, why not today? Why not now?

Forgiven

Forgiven means "to do something pleasant or agreeable (to one), to do a favour to, show one's self gracious, kind, benevolent, to pardon, graciously restore one to another, to preserve for one a person in peril."

Friends, please slowly reread each of those definitions. Meditate on the fact that God did us a favor! God chose to be benevolent to us. We were in peril of hell. How could a just God forgive us in light of our sin debt? He couldn't if Jesus hadn't died on the Cross for our sins (Colossians 2:13–14).

20. Fill in the blanks that explain how your forgiveness was obtained. Replace the word *us* with *me*. (Colossians 2:14)

He "______________________ out the certificate of debt consisting of decrees against __________ and which was ______________ to ______________; and He has taken it ______________ of the way, having ______________ it to the cross."

Jesus paid our sin debt. Paul, in his heartfelt attempt to help us understand the breadth of what God and Christ did for us, uses the following illustrations.

God Canceled Our Certificate of Debt

In Colossians 2:14, Paul refers to our certificate of debt. A certificate of debt was a note signed by a debtor acknowledging his indebtedness. It was much like an IOU. We're conscious of sin through the Ten Commandments and also because God's written His law on our hearts (Romans 2:14–15). Each time we sin it's entered on our certificate of debt. The good news is that God canceled, "anointed, washed in every part, wiped off, wiped away, obliterated, erased, blotted out" our certificate of debt. How could that be?

In ancient days, documents were written on either papyrus made from a bulrush type of plant or on vellum made from animal skin. The papers didn't absorb ink as ours do today. Therefore a scribe could use a sponge to *wipe off* or could scrape off words written on the paper when it was no longer needed. This visual lesson helps us understand what God did with our sin debt. When we confess our sins, God is faithful and just to forgive our sins and cleanse us from all unrighteousness. God wipes away our sins and it appears they never happened. What a great God we have! What grace! What mercy!

21. How do you feel knowing that God wiped away, blotted out all your sins with Christ's blood? ____

God Nailed Our Certificate of Debt to the Cross

Paul used a second illustration to help us understand that salvation isn't dependent on our external legalistic rites or good works. God accomplished our salvation and it's complete in Christ.

22. What happened to our certificate of debt according to Colossians 2:14?

Our certificate of debt was nailed to Jesus's cross. Our sin was credited to Him. Our sins were transferred from our sinful back to Jesus's holy back. He took our sin to Golgotha, wiped it out, and when Jesus died and was buried, so was our sin. When Jesus was raised in power and glory, so were we! As 2 Corinthians 5:21 beautifully states, "He [God] made Him [Christ] who knew no sin to be sin on our behalf, so that we might become the righteousness of God in Him."

Does physical circumcision save? No. Do good works save? No. Does following church tradition save? No. Does water baptism save? No.

23. By what means are we saved? (Ephesians 2:8–9) ________________________

What's in Your Basket?

Basket Case

- Try to please God by laws and traditions
- Don't believe God's forgiven all my sin
- Bound by traditions

Extraordinary Life

- Live by the Spirit
- Praise God for forgiving all my sin
- Freed to live for Christ

♦ *Perhaps I'm a basket case because I worry about my salvation. I try to legalistically follow man's traditions rather than praise God for my salvation.*

♦ *Perhaps I'm a basket case because I'm controlling. I want others to follow my traditions.*

♦ *Perhaps I'm a basket case because I focus more on my flesh than on Christ in me.*

♦ *Perhaps I'm a basket case because I live buried in sin rather than walk in newness of life.*

Thinking It Over

♥ 1. How could adhering to legalism cause someone to live a basket-case life instead of an extraordinary life for Christ?

____

____

♥ 2. Why is Paul's warning about legalism important to the church today?

____

____

♥ 3. Which illustration of salvation best helps you understand what God did for you when He saved you? Practice explaining it.

____

____

♥ 4. What do you want to remember from today's lesson?

____

____

♥ 5. Thank God for wiping away your sins and making you alive in Christ.

____

____

Day 5: *Mysticism and Asceticism*

Lord, thank You for purchasing my salvation with Christ's blood. Thank You for taking my sins to the Cross. There is no way I can repay You. Yet I can offer my life to You. Please take it and use it to bring glory to Your name. In Jesus's name. Amen.

◆ ◆ ◆

Mary's father was overjoyed. Paul's explanation of circumcision ended his indecisiveness about whether or not he needed the procedure. He was now fully assured his salvation was complete in Christ.

◆ ◆ ◆

"In Christ." The words rang through Mary's ears as she dipped the family's dirty clothes into the wash bucket and rinsed them clean. "My heart... cleansed. Forgiven. Buried with Christ. Raised to newness of life," Mary rejoiced.

◆ ◆ ◆

Paul woke early to continue his letter to the believers. Today, he knew he must address the false teachings of mysticism and asceticism that had crept into the church.

◆ ◆ ◆

Rulers and Authorities

Read Colossians 2:10–15.

Throughout his letter, Paul exalts Christ as Lord over all.

1. What has Paul stated about Christ in relation to rule and authority? (Colossians 2:10)

____

____

Rulers can either be a reference to human leaders or angels and demons. *Authorities* refers to "the power of rule or government."

2. In addition to Jesus being over all rule and authority, what did God do to rulers and authorities?
   God: ❑ Disarmed rulers and authorities. ❑ Made a public display of them.
   ❑ Triumphed over them.

3. Through whom or by what power did God disarm the rulers and authorities, make a public display of them, and triumphed over them? ____________________

____

Some scholars believe this is a reference to Jesus in relation to angels and demons. Others believe it's a reference to Jesus in relation to the authorities responsible for His crucifixion. Personally, I believe it applies to both.

Disarmed

In Colossians 2:15, Paul proclaims Christ in a way that should affect our lives. *Disarmed* is the word used for stripping weapons and armor from a defeated enemy. When Jesus rose from the grave, He stripped Satan of the weapon of death. In other words, Jesus stripped Satan of sin's power to separate us from God. Jesus stripped Jews and Romans of their lies that Jesus wasn't the Son of the Living God! Praise be to God! Jesus stripped Satan of his power over us. As Warren Wiersbe stated in *The Bible Exposition Commentary*, "Satan cannot harm the believer who will not harm himself. It is when we cease to watch and pray (as did Peter) that Satan can use his weapons against us."

Displayed

Display means "to make an example of, to show as an example." Jesus made a public spectacle of the Jewish and Roman authorities as well as of the devil and his angels. Jesus had told them He was God. He explained He'd come from heaven and was returning. He told Pilate He had no authority except what God gave Him. He told everyone He'd rise three days after His death. Anyone who denies what Christ states will be publicly displayed as wrong—if not in this lifetime, in the next.

Triumphed

Triumphed means "celebrated. It's from a root word meaning a hymn sung in festal processions in honor of the god Bacchus," the Greek god of wine. When the Colossians heard that "Jesus triumphed," it would have called to mind triumphant Roman generals marching armies through the arch in Rome, followed by defeated captives. Here Paul pictures Christ as the triumphant, conquering King. In the wake is Satan and his defeated army of demons.

The Christian's ability to live victoriously is grounded in Christ who triumphed over Satan. Perhaps if I'm a basket case, it's because I yield to Satan's temptations rather than victoriously stand against them in the triumphant name of Jesus.

Legalism . . . Shadows or Substance?

Read Colossians 2:16–17.

After explaining why Jesus is the head over all rule and authority, heavenly and earthly, Paul addresses specific issues believers face.

4. List the issues Paul addresses in Colossians 2:16–17. ______________________

____

In these verses, Paul explains how Old Testament traditions and laws that foreshadowed Christ are no longer needed because Christ fulfilled them. Christians are free from Old Testament eating requirements (Acts 10:9–15; Romans 14:1–4; 1 Timothy 4:1–4). Christians aren't bound to keep Jewish festivals such as the new moon celebration or Sabbath day.

5. Rather than the kingdom of God being based on Jewish eating and drinking laws, how does Romans 14:17 describe the kingdom of God? ____________________

____

♦ *Perhaps I'm a basket case because I live under the shadow of ceremonies and mere religious rituals without the substance of righteousness, peace, and joy in Christ.*

Mysticism

Read Colossians 2:18–19.

"Mysticism is the belief a person can have an immediate experience with the spiritual world, completely apart from the Word of God or the Holy Spirit," says Warren Wiersbe in *The Bible Exposition Commentary*. Mysticism is forbidden because people who bypass the Word of God and Spirit of God open themselves to demonic spirits (Deuteronomy 18:10–13; Isaiah 8:19). In this passage, Paul warns Christians not to be involved with mysticism, speculations, and beliefs that have no sound basis in Christ.

6. What is Paul's concern in Colossians 2:18? ____________________

____

Defraud here means "to beguile of the prize of victory." In other words, Paul's concern is, if Christians follow false teachers, they'll get caught up in things that divert them from the good works God prepared for them to do (Ephesians 2:8–10). If that happens, they'll miss the rewards Christ has for them.

7. Check two teachings Paul warned them not to follow.
   - ❑ Worship of angels ❑ Taking a stand on visions
   - ❑ Being filled with the Holy Spirit

This is an interesting passage and very applicable! I remember numerous occasions when someone purported to see a vision that later proved a hoax. For instance, in 1985, a painting of the Virgin Mary at a monastery in Texas was purported to cry tears of oil. However, in 2006, a monk from the monastery admitted the painting was a hoax. In the meantime, people flocked to see the vision of the "crying Mary."

8. What does the spiritually minded person do rather than seek angels and visions? (Colossians 2:19) ______________________________

____

Spiritually minded people hold fast to Jesus, not visions or angels, whom believers are forbidden to worship (Exodus 20:3–5; Revelation 22:8–9). Spiritually minded people grow because they open their minds and hearts to Christ's Spirit, who flows through them and supplies them with His divine nature (2 Peter 1:3–4).

Dear sisters, as the worship of angels, intermediaries, and seeking visions increases in our society, we must be on guard. Those led astray will try to convince us to discover "higher" enlightenment. Colossians forewarns us to seek Christ alone.

- *Perhaps I'm a basket case because I delight in false humility. Rather than take Jesus at His word and pray directly to God, I pray through intermediaries.*
- *Perhaps I'm a basket case because I seek spirituality through angels and visions rather than hold to Jesus through Bible study and prayer.*
- *Perhaps I'm a basket case because I seek visions rather than Christ.*

Asceticism . . . Dead or Alive to Christ?

Read Colossians 2:20–23.

According to *The Bible Knowledge Commentary*, *asceticism* "is the pseudo-spiritual position that revels in rules of physical self-denial."

9. What warning does Paul give in this passage? ______________________________

____

____

Wuest's Word Studies from the Greek New Testament for the English Reader tells us,

> These prohibitions relate to defilement contrasted in diverse ways by contact with impure objects. Some were doubtless reenactments of the Mosaic law, while others would be exaggerations or additions of a rigorous asceticism, such as we find among the Essene prototypes of these Colossian heretics, e.g. the avoidance of oil, of wine, or of flesh-meat, the shunning of contact with a stranger or a religious inferior, and the like.

10. What is Paul's argument for why Christians shouldn't adhere to such false teachings?

a) Colossians 2:20 ______________________________

b) Colossians 2:23 ______________________________

Paul explains that Christians have died to elementary principles of the world. Our spirituality isn't based on a list of do's and don'ts, but is based on the Lord Jesus Christ. Paul also explains man-made practices have no value against fleshly indulgences. Self-control is a fruit of the Spirit (Galatians 5:22).

Ascetics practice self-mortification and self-denial based on man-made rules in an attempt to become more spiritual. Ascetics fail to recognize Jesus's teaching in Mark 7:14–23. "Do you not understand that whatever goes into a man from the outside cannot defile him?" (Mark 7:18).

As with those who practice mysticism and legalism, those who practice asceticism may give a false impression of being more spiritual than others. However, bodily discipline doesn't sanctify a person's soul.

Rather, let those of us whose souls are sanctified by Jesus discipline our bodies because we understand they're temples of the Holy Spirit (1 Corinthians 6:19). As Spirit-filled Christians, let us eat and drink as unto the Lord, with a good conscience (Romans 14:13–23).

What's in Your Basket?

Basket Case

- Live in the shadow of the Law
- Seek forbidden spiritual experiences
- Try to please God by self-abasement

Extraordinary Life

- Live in the substance of Christ and His grace
- Seek spiritual experiences in Christ, through God's Word and Holy Spirit
- Discipline my body because it's the temple of the Holy Spirit

- ♦ *Perhaps I'm a basket case because I submit myself to man-made religion or self-abasement in an effort to please God.*
- ♦ *Perhaps I'm a basket case because I yield to Satan rather than stand victoriously against him in Jesus's name.*
- ♦ *Perhaps I'm a basket case because I live in the shadow of the Law rather than the substance of Christ's righteousness, peace, and joy in the Holy Spirit.*
- ♦ *Perhaps I'm a basket case because I seek visions rather than Christ.*
- ♦ *Perhaps I'm a basket case because I seek enlightenment apart from God, the Bible, and God's Spirit.*

Thinking It Over

♥ 1. Which of Paul's warnings today are most relevant to:

Society:

You:

♥ 2. What are your feelings about seeking spiritual things apart from the Bible and Holy Spirit? What danger is there in bypassing the Word and Spirit of God?

♥ 3. How would you explain the difference between self-discipline for the sake of Christ and ascetic practices of self-abasement and severe treatment of the body?

♥ 4. How does Jesus's triumphant victory over Satan affect your prayer life and your stand against temptation? Pray about an area of your life in which God wants to give you victory.

Weekly Wrap-Up

Where Am I? With which basket-case point do I most relate?

____

____

____

Where Do I Want to Be? To which aspects of extraordinary living is God calling me?

____

____

____

How Will I Get There? What golden nugget and/or verse do I want to remember to help me better handle my basket-case moments and live an extraordinary life?

____

____

____

Thinking of Others: What from this week's study do I want to share with someone to encourage or warn them?

____

____

____

Congratulations on a week well done! We're halfway through our study. I pray God is richly blessing you!

◆ Week 5 ◆

DOWN IN THE DUMPS OR REVELING IN CHRIST'S GLORY?

In Colossians 3, we learn that if we want to live extraordinary lives for God, it begins with where we set our minds.

◆ ◆ ◆

The morning was hot, humid, and stifling. On top of that, the soldier who stood guard was gruff and out of sorts. Looking at his chains, Paul wished he could will them away. In that moment of chains, humidity, and the unpleasant guard, Paul's spirit was stirred, "Come to Me." Turning from his circumstances, over which he had no control, Paul set his mind and thoughts on Jesus, His risen Lord.

◆ ◆ ◆

Mary thought she was going to explode! Her little brother seemed to take pleasure in annoying her while she did her chores. Wiping the sweat from her brow, she swept the floor and straightened the beds. "It's not going to be a good day!" Mary mumbled to herself.

◆ ◆ ◆

Day 1: *Seek the Things Above*

Father, so often I become overwhelmed with earthly things. Teach me to see all my circumstances from Your perspective. Help me set my eyes on You. I love You and thank You. In Jesus's name. Amen.

Years ago, Pam Kanaly, one of my college roommates and a dear friend, told me she was going to memorize Colossians 3, and asked if I would join her. I agreed, but was a bit overwhelmed at the idea. I had memorized select verses and even passages, but never a whole chapter. To be honest, I wasn't even sure why I needed to memorize Colossians 3:11, "Barbarian, Scythian, slave and freeman." Regardless, I resolutely joined her!

Pam encouraged me to get a spiral notebook and to diagram or draw pictures of the verses, in order to provide a visual of what I was memorizing. I still have that notebook. Each week, we memorized a few verses and called each other to hold each other accountable. Words can't express how grateful I am to Pam for challenging me to memorize Colossians 3. In the last 25 years, God has often brought these verses to my mind, especially verses 1–2. When He does, I'm reminded to turn my mind and heart to Him in prayer. I'm reminded to look up at His glorious throne, to consider whatever is happening to me or around me from His divine viewpoint. I encourage you to memorize Colossians 3.

Read Colossians 3:1–3.

1. How does Colossians 3:1 begin?
   - ❑ Put on the full armor of God
   - ❑ Whatever you do in word or deed, do all in the name of the Lord Jesus
   - ❑ Therefore

Any time we read the word *therefore* in the Bible, it is *there for* a reason. *Therefore* is a word that means "for that reason," "because," "consequently."

In reading Paul's letter, it helps to remember he didn't divide his letter into segments; it was one continuous letter. What Paul says in Colossians 3:1 is in the same breath as Colossians 2:23.

2. What has Paul been saying in chapters 1–2? Draw a line to match the chapter number on the left with its content in the right-hand column.

Colossians 1	Let no one delude you, act as your judge in regard to food or drink, or defraud you of your prize because in Jesus all the fullness of deity dwells in bodily form. In Him you have been made complete. In Him you were buried and raised; made alive together with Christ. God has forgiven all your transgressions.
Colossians 2	Jesus is the exalted Son of God, Creator, the believer's hope of glory, who mightily works within the believer.

Chapter 3 begins the ethical, instructive part of Paul's letter in which he essentially says, "Because of who Christ is and your identification with Him, this is how you can and should live."

3. Paul has discussed numerous aspects of what we have in Christ, and what to guard against. What is at the forefront of his mind in Colossians 3:1?
   - ❑ Not letting anyone defraud us
   - ❑ Devoting ourselves to prayer
   - ❑ We've been raised up with Christ

4. This is the third time Paul has told us that we've been raised up with Christ. When was the first time? Record the chapter and verse. ______________________

5. Paul repeats and reminds. What words does he use to express the same concept?

____

____

"Raised up with Christ," "made... alive together with Him" are revolutionary spiritual concepts! The teaching that Christians are identified with Jesus in His death, burial, resurrection, and ascension is called the doctrine of identification. When we begin understanding our identification in Christ, our attitudes and lives become infused with Christ's perspective and power.

6. Where is Christ? (Colossians 3:1) ______________________

Christ has returned to His former glory. He is seated, indicating His work is complete. He is at God the Father's right hand, a position of power and authority.

When I was a little girl, I heard someone speak of salvation as being when God forgives you of your sins and Jesus comes into your heart. I immediately visualized a miniature Jesus coming into my heart. Although it's true Jesus comes into our hearts through the Holy Spirit at salvation, the resurrected Lord Jesus Christ is *seated* bodily at the right hand of God in majesty (Hebrews 8:1).

7. What does Paul conclude based on all he's explained in Colossians 1–2? Complete Colossians 3:1. "Therefore if [since] you have been raised up with Christ...

____

____

____

We can almost hear Paul reasoning with us, "Accepting Christ is just the beginning of your new life! Don't stop! Keep going! Keep seeking the things above where Christ is!"

Seek

In this passage, *seek* means "to seek in order to find or to find out by thinking, meditating, reasoning; to strive after, crave." Do you strive after the things above? Do you crave Jesus? The verb tense for *seek* is the present imperative active tense.

- It is a *command* to continuously seek.
- It is a command to *keep on* seeking *as your general habit or lifestyle.*
- It's a *commitment* to a long-term way of doing something.

8. What are you to keep seeking? (Colossians 3:1) ______________________

Things Above

Above here means "on high." Paul explains that, since we've been crucified, buried, and raised with Christ, we should continuously think on our higher calling in Christ. We should imitate Jesus and seek things that glorify God (John 1:14; 8:29; 17:22). We should crave Christ and the things of God.

Read the following characteristics of believers who seek the things above and thus glorify God. Check those you need to seek to do.

- ❑ I view sin as part of my old nature, crucified with Christ. I view myself as dead to it.
- ❑ I view my relationships from Christ's perspective. I raise children to know the Lord. I model Christ to less mature believers. I'm a peacemaker in the midst of strife. I pray for and witness to unsaved friends.
- ❑ I view my purpose in life as living for Christ, not myself.
- ❑ I view my money and possessions as that which God has entrusted to me. My money and possessions are not mine.
- ❑ I view my service to God on the basis of Christ's power in me, not my ability.
- ❑ I view difficult, dark times as opportunities in which I can be a vessel of Christ's Light.

Because of our identification with Christ, we can and should seek Christ and the calling to "things above."

Did you ever play "hide-and-seek"? Although it's a fun childhood game, it doesn't apply to Christ and us. He isn't hidden, as Gnostics teach. Jesus isn't playing a game of "hide-and-seek." He told the disciples where He was going (John 16:28). They watched Jesus ascend to heaven (Acts 1:9–11). Now, Paul writes, "Keep seeking the things above, where Christ is, seated at the right hand of God" (Colossians 3:1).

9. Look up the following Scriptures that speak of "seeking" in relation to the Father, the Son, the Holy Spirit, and the devil.

   a) What instruction about "seeking" does Jesus give? (Matthew 6:33–34)

   ____

   ____

   b) What type of worshipper is God seeking? (John 4:23) ______________

   ____

   ____

   c) What is the devil seeking? (1 Peter 5:8) ______________

   d) What are you seeking? (thinking about, meditating on, striving after)

   ____

   ____

God is seeking you. So is Satan. Both crave you. God is seeking true worshippers. Satan is seeking someone to devour. Doesn't it make sense to follow Paul's advice and to be a true worshipper who seeks the things above?

What's in Your Basket?

Basket Case

- Mind on things of earth
- Seek what's best for me
- Seek my glory
- Crave things of world: power, affirmation, sex, possessions
- Continuously seek things above

Extraordinary Life

- Seek Christ's higher calling for my life
- Seek Christ's glory
- Crave Jesus and things above

- ♦ *Perhaps I'm a basket case because I've not made a long-term commitment to seeking the things above and to seeking God's higher calling for my life.*
- ♦ *Perhaps I'm a basket case because my intimacy with God is less than it should be. God seeks those who worship Him and my mind is on earthly things.*
- ♦ *Perhaps I'm a basket case because I leave myself open to Satan. I don't stand against him.*
- ♦ *Perhaps I'm a basket case because I don't seek what God wants to do in and through my life that will bring Him glory.*

Thinking It Over

♥ 1. What has God impressed on you today in Colossians 3:1? ______________________

____

____

♥ 2. What would happen if you sought Jesus's perspective on any worrisome, discouraging, unwholesome, or critical thoughts you might have? ______________________

____

____

♥ 3. What would happen if you sought to glorify Jesus in the midst of whatever caused the worrisome, discouraging, unwholesome, critical thoughts? ______________________

____

____

♥ 4. Pray about whatever is on your heart and mind. Repent if it isn't your habit to seek the things above as part of your general lifestyle. Seek His perspective on any challenging situation you're going through. ______________________________

____

____

____

DAY 2: *Set Your Mind on the Things Above*

Father, please guide my study today. Help me comprehend what You mean when You tell me to set my mind on the things above. Help me not just study Your words, but live them. Give my mind a new home . . . in You. In Jesus's name. Amen.

"Have you ever thought you were going to lose your mind?" Mary asked Eunice, a new friend she'd met at church. Walking home from the market, they'd enjoyed many good discussions. Mary felt she could confide in Eunice. In addition, Eunice always gave sound advice. "Mary, of course I do. Everyone feels stressed at times. But remember what Paul wrote?"

About that time, a woman bumped into Mary on the crowded street and sent her and her groceries tumbling to the ground. Rather than stopping and apologizing, the woman continued down the street. Eunice, who expected Mary to be upset, heard Mary quietly say to herself, "Seek the things above where Christ is."

"Do you know who that was?" Mary asked as she rose to her feet. "She's the spiritist who's been introducing false teachings on angelic enlightenment. Maybe God will give us another chance to 'bump' into each other so I can tell her about the true Light."

"You're not losing your mind," Eunice laughed. "You're more sound than ever!"

Paul realized it might seem to the Colossians that he was overly repetitious on some subjects. However, after visiting with Timothy and Epaphras, he felt convinced he needed to reinforce the idea that, although a believer's salvation was complete in Christ, a believer's sanctification—being set apart from sin and unto God—required practice. "You have to keep seeking," Paul explained. "You have to set your mind on the things above."

REREAD COLOSSIANS 3:1–4. I hope you're memorizing it!

Yesterday, we studied that we're to keep seeking things above. Our decision to accept Christ shouldn't be the end of our pursuit of God. Rather, it opens to us the throne room where Christ majestically sits at the right hand of God.

1. What does God command us in Colossians 3:2? ______________________________

____

____

Set

Set here means "to direct one's mind to a thing". *The Complete Word Study New Testament* explains *set your mind* implies not only thought but also "the affections, will, or moral consideration."

2. Rewrite the first part of Colossians 3:2, which says where we're to *set* our minds. Substitute the definition: "thoughts, affections, will, or moral consideration" in the place of *minds*. Write it in the first person. ______________________________

____

____

3. What difference might it make if you directed and filtered your thoughts, affections, will, and moral considerations to God before anywhere else? ______________________________

____

____

Recently, while Keith and I were on our morning walk, a less than edifying thought about someone popped in my mind. Remembering Ephesians 4:29, "Let no unwholesome word proceed from your mouth, but only such a word as is good for edification according to the need of the moment, so that it will give grace to those who hear," I decided to keep the thought to myself and not share it with Keith.

Further into our walk, the unkind thought resurfaced. Again, I wanted to share my perspective on a person that would have in no way built that person up. I put out some bait to see if Keith would bite. He didn't. Later, I brought up the topic a second time! I'm constantly amazed at God's patience toward me! By God's grace, the words about the matter didn't come out of my mouth. As I directed my mind heavenward, God continually set a guard over my mouth. He constantly asked me, "Will it build up or tear down the person? Is it truth or speculation? If speculation, then you'll be putting in Keith's mind that which may be false and is also disparaging of the person."

Setting our minds on things above, where God is, changes how we think, what we say, and what we do. For instance, we can't be unkind and at the same time have our affections set on God. We can't lie if we're looking at Jesus with our minds set on Him.

If you haven't hidden Colossians 3:2 in your heart, do so today.

4. Rewrite the last part of Colossians 3:2 which says where we're *not* to set our minds. Again, substitute the definition: "thoughts, affections, will, or moral consideration" in the place of *minds*. Write it in the first person. ______________________________

____

____

____

5. As Paul often does, he contrasts two places where we can set our minds. What opposites does he contrast?

   ❑ Heaven and hell ❑ Earth and wind ❑ Earth and above

When Paul writes we're not to set our minds on the things of earth, he isn't saying we're to ignore our earthly responsibilities. He isn't saying we're not to do the wash, make birthday cakes, clean the house, go to work, raise our children, and pay the bills. As a matter of fact, the rest of Colossians 3 deals with earthly relationships—marriage, parenting, and work ethics.

Earth in this context, is contrasted with heaven. It's associated with emptiness, weakness, and sinfulness; not the wisdom and power of God. Christians have been purchased from the earth. One day we'll be resurrected from it. In the meantime, we're to set our minds on the things above it.

Since our minds, thoughts, affections, will, and moral beliefs affect our behavior, it's imperative we take proactive measures not to absorb earth's values, perspectives, and weaknesses, but rather to absorb heaven's.

Proactive Ways to Set Our Minds on the Things Above

Read Romans 12:1–2

6. Romans 12:1–2 details how we can set our minds on the things above and be transformed into Christ's image rather than be conformed to the world. Read Romans 12:1–2, and then fill in the following blanks.

   a) We can set our minds on the things above by ______________________ our bodies as living and holy sacrifices to God.

Every day we wake and meet with God, we're choosing to set our minds on the things above. That's a positive first step!

As Christians, we're called to offer our bodies to God as living sacrifices. Although we've been positionally "crucified with Christ," we're not yet in the grave. Therefore, as those alive in Christ, we're able to use our bodies to serve God. We set our minds on the things above by offering our affections, our thoughts, our will, and our moral considerations to God instead of being absorbed with the temporal things of the world.

b) We can set our minds on the things above by ______________________ and renewing our minds according to God's Word.

When we expose our minds to God's will and ways, our minds become transformed. Just as a person begins mimicking those he or she spends a lot of time around, we become more like Jesus the more we're around Him in His Word. When you walk with Jesus through the Bible, when you hear His Words, commands, and promises, you're setting your mind on Him. Your mind is being renewed. Need a new mind? Need new thoughts? Then act like a sponge and soak in and soak up God's Word and ways.

7. How do we set our minds on the things above when we're not reading our Bible or praying? Thoughtfully answer the following questions.

   a) While ironing, cooking, or relaxing, do you watch shows that are wholesome or unwholesome; support God's ways or reflect earth's wrong values?

____

____

   b) While driving carpool, visiting on the phone, or sitting at lunch, do you speak whatever comes to your mind even if it's not wholesome? Or do you set your mind on verses like Ephesians 4:29 and guard your mouth?

____

____

   c) While caring for the sick, housebound, or difficult, do you allow your mind to run amok with resentment, pity, anger, or despair? Or do you set your mind on the things above and pray for wisdom, love, and patience?

____

____

   d) When enjoying downtime, do you set your mind on Christian music, teachings, books, or talk shows that strengthen your inner man? Or do you set your mind on books, music, or conversation that kindle discontentment and temptation?

____

____

Setting my mind on the things above is a *choice*. It's something I can control. It's God's command to me for my edification and His glory.

When Pam and I memorized Colossians 3, I vividly remember the visual God gave me to help me memorize these verses. I thought of how I take plates from the kitchen cabinet and set them on the table. There are several points we can glean as we make the spiritual application.

There is nothing evil about my kitchen cabinets. Likewise, Paul isn't taking a Gnostic position and stating the earth (flowers, trees, hills, and streams) is evil. Everything God created is good (Genesis 1:31; 1 Timothy 4:4–5). However, my plates weren't purchased to sit in the cabinet. They were purchased to be set on the table and to serve food. In like manner, God didn't purchase us merely to sit on earth. He wants to use us to serve heavenly blessings to others.

Setting the table requires purposeful action. Cups and plates don't move to the table on their own. Neither do our minds initially move on their own toward the things above. We make a choice to set our minds on God when we wake in the mornings, are running late for work, balancing the checkbook, bouncing the baby on our hip while making peanut butter sandwiches, lifting a wheelchair in the car, scheduling doctor's appointments, and handing out medicine, and so on. When we purposefully set our minds on the things above in the midst of our daily routines, we're able to live out our responsibilities with God's perspective, power, and discipline. This is the extraordinary life, sisters.

READ 2 CORINTHIANS 10:3–5.

There's another proactive way we can set our minds on the things above. In 2 Corinthians Paul addresses the problem of spiritual battles. He uses military terms: *wars, weapons,* and *fortresses*. No doubt, living under house arrest in Rome provided Paul a visual of spiritual warfare. Paul states in 2 Corinthians 10:3–5 that, though we walk in the flesh, we don't war according to the flesh. He then directs us to powerful, divine weapons we have. Guess where these weapons are found? Not on the earth. In heaven.

8. What does Paul say can be destroyed when we set our minds above, on the divinely powerful weapons of prayer, faith, hope, love, and righteousness? (2 Corinthians 10:4–5)
   ❑ Fortresses ❑ Speculations
   ❑ Lofty things raised up against the knowledge of God

God's enemy, Satan, blinds unbelievers to the truth. Satan accuses Christians. However, when we set our minds on the things above through prayer—when we ask God to fill us with His Spirit—and we walk accordingly, Satan's strongholds and accusations are destroyed! Praise be to God!

9. There's a final thought in 2 Corinthians 10:5 regarding our minds being set on the things above. On occasion we may have thoughts that aren't true, about ourselves, a situation, or even others. For instance,
   - Satan made Eve doubt God. (Genesis 3:1–5)
   - Ananias and Sapphira "thought" they could deceive Peter, lie to the Holy Spirit, and not suffer the consequences. (Acts 5:1–10)

- A Christian can think another Christian is sinning; yet the accused may have a clean conscience before God. (Romans 14)

10. What does 2 Corinthians 10:5 instruct us to do with our minds, speculations, and thoughts?
    - ❑ Let my thoughts run loose.
    - ❑ Take my thoughts captive to the obedience of Christ.

Friends, we can set our minds on the things above by offering our minds and bodies to God. We can set our minds on the things above by taking our thoughts captive to God and filtering them through Him and the Bible.

What's in Your Basket?

Basket Case

- Forget to set my mind on things above
- Entertain thoughts of anger and resentment
- Soak up worldly culture
- Direct my mind to earthy talk shows and movies
- Set my mind on my interests, not God's
- Let my thoughts run wild

Extraordinary Life

- Set my mind on things above
- Offer my mind, body, thoughts to God
- Soak up God's Word and ways
- Direct my thoughts to that which edifies others and brings glory to God
- Set my mind on God's interests
- Take my thoughts captive to God

- ♦ *Perhaps I'm a basket case because I don't set my mind on the things above, where Christ is.*
- ♦ *Perhaps I'm a basket case because I direct my mind to "earthy" things. I watch television shows and read books that make me unhappy with my life and stir wrong imaginations.*
- ♦ *Perhaps I'm a basket case because I set my mind on my interests, not God's.*
- ♦ *Perhaps I'm a basket case because I let my thoughts run wild instead of taking them captive to God.*
- ♦ *Perhaps I'm a basket case because I've never gone through the crisis of decision and truly set my mind on being transformed. I've never offered my body and mind to God.*

Thinking It Over

♥ 1. How is God speaking to you through Colossians 3:2?

___

♥ 2. If you've never committed to setting your mind on the things above, will you prayerfully do so now? ___

♥ 3. What does God want you to take your mind *from* in order to set it *on* Him? What sin, temptation, habit, or thought do you need to take captive to Christ?

___

♥ 4. What golden nugget do you want to remember from today's lesson?

___

DAY 3: *You Have Died*

Father, Your Word is rich and deep. Help me comprehend what being identified with You in death and life means. In Jesus's name. Amen.

♦ ♦ ♦

Walking to the well, Mary pondered Paul's words. "Keep seeking the things above, where Christ is, seated at the right hand of God. Set your mind on the things above, not on the things that are on earth." Puzzled, she wondered how she could keep up with her earthly responsibilities and at the same time seek the things above. It was then she recognized she was doing the very thing she wanted. She was setting her mind on the things above by meditating on God's Word. Laughing at herself, Mary asked God to continue to teach her how to set her mind on the things above.

♦ ♦ ♦

Paul longed for the believers in Colossae to understand the fullness of life they had in Christ. Prayerfully, he sought God's direction for how to best word the teachings, that believers are dead to sin and alive with Christ in God!

♦ ♦ ♦

Reread Colossians 3:1–3.

Yesterday we studied that we're to set our mind on the things above, not on the things on earth.

1. What two reasons does Paul give for why we should set our thoughts, affections, will, and moral consideration above instead of on the earth? Please answer in the first person if you are a Christian.

   a) ____

   b) ____

You Have Died

Recently a dear friend, Glen McGinnis, died. His death was sudden. He went for a walk, had a massive heart attack, and never returned to his physical home. Rather, he went to his eternal home.

When a friend called and said, "Glen's died," I couldn't believe it. You may have received such a call and know the shock of hearing those words. Although those who die in Christ are alive in heaven, they are dead to this earth. In other words, a dead person isn't stimulated or tempted by the things of earth.

In the same sense, a person who has been crucified and raised with Christ is dead to the things of earth and alive to things of God. In using this metaphor, Paul helps us understand what happens at our salvation. The person you were when you were physically born undergoes change. The old-natured unbeliever is viewed as dead. At salvation you become a new, regenerated creation (Titus 3:5) with a new nature.

What kind of death is Paul talking about? Obviously we're not physically dead! Neither are we spiritually dead. We are more spiritually alive than ever. We're not emotionally or intellectually dead.

2. Read the following Scriptures and record that to which you're dead.

   1 Peter 2:24 ____________________________________

   Romans 6:2 ____________________________________

When Paul tells us as believers we've died and are to consider ourselves dead to sin, *dead* means "inactive." Death means separation, not extinction. To be dead to sin is to be separated from the ruling power of sin in one's life (Romans 6:14).

3. Paul communicates the concept of being dead to sin in Romans 6:11. Write out this verse in the first person. ____________________________

____

____

Consider means "to reckon or calculate." It is an accounting term. "Add it up, 1-2-3," Paul seems to say:

a) Our old self was crucified with Christ so that our "body of sin" might be disempowered and we'd no longer be slaves to sin (Romans 6:6).

b) Dead people are free from sin. They aren't aroused by sin (Romans 6:7).

c) We're dead because we were crucified with Christ. God let Christ's death count for us (Romans 6:8).

Paul then explains how we can avoid stimulating our dead sin nature.

4. Record Paul's three-point advice for remaining separate from (dead to) the power of sin.

   Do not: (Romans 6:12) ______________________________

   ____

   Do not: (Romans 6:13) ______________________________

   ____

   Do: (Romans 6:13) ______________________________

   ____

Do Not Let Sin Reign

Reign means "be king, rule, have predominance." Don't let sin have power, dominance, or control. Don't obey sin's lusts.

We all know what Paul's talking about. Whether you have a problem with worry, anxiousness, pride, lust, lying, procrastination, gossip, abusing alcohol or other drugs, immorality, or with your thought life, you know there's a moment of choice when you either say no to the temptation or you yield your body and mind to the sin and give it power, dominance, and control over you. Every time we give in to sin and obey its lust, we fan the flame and give life to the sin. We literally keep the sin alive.

5. For your eyes only, what sin tries to reign in you or control your thoughts or actions?

   ____

   ____

   ____

Do Not Go on Presenting the Members of Your Body to Sin

Paul says don't continue in the way you've been going in regard to sin. Don't go on presenting or yielding the members of your body to sin as instruments of unrighteousness. Don't let the devil play you like a fiddle! To present or yield means to give in to. Don't just stand there and let Satan use you as an instrument of unrighteousness! Don't let him use your mind, heart, arms, legs, or eyes for his evil purposes. Be dead to Satan! Be dead to sin. Don't look at, taste, feel, think, entertain, or act on his temptations. Run from them. Separate from them! Christ has won the battle over the devil and sin. Sin has no power over you except what you give it.

6. For your eyes only, what member of your body does Satan want to use as an instrument of unrighteousness? ______________________________

Present Yourself to God and Your Members as Instruments of Righteousness

Present yourself to God as those who are alive from the dead. Sisters, God's equipped us to use us in His kingdom. We are to present (yield) our members: our hands, eyes, mind, arms, feet, and hearts to God as instruments of righteousness. Perhaps we need to say to our enemy, "These things—my arms, mouth, eyes, mind—are *dead* to you, Satan, ole foe. You can't have them or use them! I've given them to God!"

By doing so, we're available to yield, and be ready for God to use us. Do you need to say to Christ, "I'm alive thanks to You, Lord Jesus! Need a pair of legs to take the gospel to someone? I'm Your go-to girl! Need someone to read and study the Bible to prepare the next generation to take the gospel to their friends? I'm right here, Lord. I'm available for You to use me any way, any time, anywhere!"?

7. Let's go back and reread Colossians 3:2–3 in light of what we've studied. How would you explain to someone the meaning of Colossians 3:3, "For you have died".

____

____

What's in Your Basket?

Basket Case

- Alive to sin
- Present (yield) the members of my body to sin as instruments of unrighteousness
- Let sin reign, control, have power
- Fan sin's lusts

Extraordinary Life

- Dead to sin
- Present (yield) the members of my body to God as instruments of righteousness
- Don't let sin reign, control, have power
- Extinguish sin's lusts

♦ *Perhaps I'm a basket case because I let sin have control and power over me, although Christ defeated sin on the Cross.*

- ♦ *Perhaps I'm a basket case because I present the members of my body to sin as instruments of unrighteousness and unknowingly keep the sin alive. I fan sin's flame.*
- ♦ *Perhaps I'm a basket case because I don't present the members of my body to God as one alive from the dead. I fail to present the members of my body to God as instruments of righteousness.*

Thinking It Over

♥ 1. How is God speaking to you through Colossians 3:3 and your study of what it means to be dead to sin? ____

____

____

____

♥ 2. What member of your body have you let sin use as an instrument of unrighteousness? Do your eyes look at things they shouldn't? Does your heart covet? Does sin use your mind as a hothouse in which he plants seeds of bitterness? Is your tongue a clamoring instrument of unrighteousness? Is sin using your hands to visit Web sites that are unwholesome or waste precious time God could use? Is sin using your feet to take you places you should avoid? ____

____

____

____

♥ 3. How is God waking you to the fact that sin has no power or control over you except what you give it? ____

____

____

____

♥ 4. How do you think God wants to use the members of your body for righteousness?

____

____

____

♥ 5. Record your thoughts and prayer to God. ____

____

____

____

Day 4: *Your Life Is Hidden with Christ*

Father, today, please help me comprehend what "your life is hidden with Christ in God" means. In Jesus's name. Amen.

◆ ◆ ◆

Mary was overjoyed with all she was learning! True, part of Paul's letter was convicting. Sometimes, she felt a stab of guilt when she realized she'd fanned sin's flame. However, she was not condemned. She wanted to grow spiritually. She wanted to learn more about God. She hungered to better understand her new kingdom life!

◆ ◆ ◆

It had been a good day. Paul climbed into bed and thought back on those God had brought to his small apartment. It amazed him that, though his body was confined, it didn't keep him from sharing Christ. Those who sought him to learn more about Jesus were true seekers. "The same is true of those who seek You, Lord Jesus. Those who want to find You will seek You. You'll let them find You." Closing his eyes and with a smile on his face, Paul drifted to sleep.

◆ ◆ ◆

Reread Colossians 3:1–4. (Do you have it memorized yet?)

1. In Colossians 3:3, Paul gives two reasons why believers should set their thoughts, affections, will, and moral consideration above instead of on earth. Yesterday we studied the first reason. What was it? ______________________________

____

2. What is the second reason we should set our minds on the things above?

____

____

Your Life Is Hidden with Christ

Believers should set their minds on the things above because their life is hidden with Christ in God.

Paul has just explained, "You have died" (Colossians 3:3). How is it, then, he now speaks of our lives? Do dead people live? Absolutely! We who are separated from sin's power are raised to new life in Christ!

3. How does Jesus describe the life He gives us?

   John 10:10 ____

____

John 10:28 ____

____

Abundant, eternal life is different from physical, worldly life. According to *The Exhaustive Concordance of the Bible*, *life*, as used in this passage, is defined: "the state of one who is possessed of vitality or is animate." It is a reference to:

> Absolute fullness of life, both essential and ethical, which belongs to God. It is life real and genuine, a life active and vigorous, devoted to God, blessed in this world of those who put their trust in Christ, but after the resurrection to be consummated by a more perfect body, to last forever.

4. Where does Paul explain that this fullness of life is found?
   - ❑ In the earth ❑ In things
   - ❑ In possessions ❑ With Christ in God

Our ultimate life—that which spiritually enlivens and animates us—isn't found in a person, job, child, home, or anything else. It's found in Christ. This is a difficult concept to understand. Actually, I'm not sure it can be understood. I believe it has to be experienced. For instance, someone might describe the exuberance of skydiving but, unless we skydive, we won't experience it for ourselves.

How can you experience fullness of life with Christ? In the same way you experience salvation—by faith. You choose to believe and act on the words of God.

God calls us into a life-changing relationship with Him. The abundant life for which we thirst is God-given. Satisfaction for our thirst for an abundant life is found in Christ alone (John 7:37–39).

5. Do you long for more in life? May I suggest you tell Christ you want to know Him more fully *and* you want to live more fully for Him? Tell Him you want to experience the life God raised you to live with Christ. Then, step out in faith and obedience. It's then you'll experience fullness of life in Christ! Express your intentions.

____

____

Hidden

Hide is a verb that means "to conceal." How incredible it is that our life is hidden with Christ—and of all places, in God! Consider the following aspects about being hidden with Christ.

a) The Greeks commonly spoke of someone who was dead and buried as being *physically hidden in the earth.* Christians, identified in Christ's death, are *spiritually hidden in Christ.*

b) False teachers called their books of so-called wisdom *apokruphoi*, the books that were *hidden* from all except those who were initiated. William Barclay says in *The Letters to the Philippians, Colossians, and Thessalonians* that Paul uses a wordplay as if to say, "For you the treasures of wisdom are hidden in your secret books; for us Christ is the treasury of wisdom and we are hidden in Him."

c) A third aspect of our being hidden is in reference to our concealment and safety in Christ. Believers are safe with Christ in God. Our salvation is secure. Just as you might keep a piece of jewelry in a safe, so you are "safely" hidden with Christ in God. Paul reiterates the believer's security in Christ in his letter to the Romans.

6. Read Romans 8:35–39, and then answer the following questions.
Who can separate you from God's love? (v. 35) ________________
What can separate you from God's love? (v. 39) ________________

Though the devil may prowl like a roaring lion seeking someone to devour, and though others may seek to harm you, you're hidden and secure with Christ. No one and nothing can separate you from Christ!

d) A fourth aspect of being hidden with Christ is that the world can't see the full intimacy we enjoy with Him. Our precious times of prayer and study, when God opens our minds to His truths, are unknown to unbelievers. Intimate moments, when Christ meets us in our spirits, are hidden from the human eye.

7. Read Luke 10:21–24. This is the only time I recall reading Jesus "rejoiced greatly in the Holy Spirit." He not only rejoiced greatly, what did He say? ________________

____

____

God let the disciples see something the religious leaders didn't see: things that were hidden from their eyes because of those leaders' unbelief.

8. Read Luke 10:23. What did Jesus do? ________________

____

Think how often people in Jesus's day missed the gracious words flowing from His lips. Think how often they missed the miracles He performed. Jesus was God in their midst, but so much of what He did and said was hidden from people's eyes because of their unbelief.

e) There's a final aspect about setting our minds on the things above. Christ ascended in glory into the clouds in heaven. In our present age, we can't see Jesus with our eyes. He is visually hidden from us. However we know Him, though we cannot see Him.

Perhaps I'm a basket case because my mind and priorities are set on my earthly life rather than my hidden life with Christ. Perhaps I need to change my focus and place it on hidden treasures and fullness in Christ. Perhaps I need to take to heart Jesus's warning that I cannot serve two masters (Matthew 6:24).

9. What words of praise or confession do you have regarding your life being hidden with Christ in God? ____________________

____

With Christ in God

Have you ever wondered with whom you might go to a party, movie, dinner, or even church? Have you ever been alone and not "with" someone? Although it's sometimes good to be alone, often we long to be with someone. We long for the presence of a companion.

There are few words Paul could have written that bring more comfort than those found in Colossians 3:3. Please reread his words.

10. Where is your life? ____________________

____

____

You are not alone, nor will you *ever* be alone if you're a believer. You're with Christ, the treasure of heaven! You're Christ's bride and safe with Him.

11. What words of praise do you have for your Lord and Savior, your constant companion? ____________________

____

In John 17:21–26, Jesus's prayer to His Father before His death, Jesus articulates the vital union believers have with Him.

12. Read John 17:21–26.

Please fill in the following blanks to describe each union.

God the Father is ____________________ Jesus.

Jesus is ____________________ the Father.

Believers are ____________________ Jesus and God.

13. In John 17:24, what is Jesus's desire in relation to you? ____________________

____

____

Jesus picks you! He wants *you* to be *with* Him! I pray you realize that you were on Jesus's mind before and during His arrest, crucifixion, and ascension.

Now Jesus asks you to keep *Him* on *your* mind. "Set your mind on the things above, not on the things that are on earth," Jesus lovingly says to you. The earth will always have worries and cares, but look up. Think on, set your heart's affections on, and find your exuberance in Jesus, who opened a way for you to be with Him eternally!

What's in Your Basket?

Basket Case

- Always looking for a good time, but never satisfied
- Miss intimate, hidden times with Jesus because of busyness
- Worry about losing my salvation
- More interested in my earthly life than my hidden life with Christ
- Point others to earthly things

Extraordinary Life

- Enjoy abundant life in Christ
- Blessed by intimate, hidden times with Jesus
- Know my life's safely hidden with Christ for eternity
- Exuberant about my hidden life with Christ
- Point others to Christ

♦ *Perhaps I'm a basket case because I look for exuberance of life in earthly things rather than in Christ.*

♦ *Perhaps I'm a basket case because I think things on earth are the treasure, although they never bring lasting joy. I'm missing the hidden treasure of my relationship with Jesus.*

♦ *Perhaps I'm a basket case because I worry about being* **with** *someone on earth. Perhaps I should follow Jesus's advice not to worry, and instead, pray and seek Him first.*

♦ *Perhaps I'm a basket case because I worry about losing my salvation. Instead, I should celebrate if I'm a Christian, because I'm with Christ in God for eternity!*

Thinking It Over

♥ 1. Look back over today's lesson. How is God speaking to you?

____

____

____

____

____

____

♥ 2. In which aspect of the extraordinary life is God prompting you to grow?

♥ 3. How might Jesus be calling you to more "hidden" times with Him?

♥ 4. For which hidden time with Jesus are you most thankful?

Day 5: *Christ, Who Is Our Life*

Father, You are a good and glorious God. From the rising of the sun to its setting, Your wonders amaze me. Your Son amazes me. Thank You for His life. In Jesus's name. Amen.

◆ ◆ ◆

Paul woke with his parents on his mind. Smiling, he fondly thought of his childhood days and how his father taught him the Jewish laws and traditions. As a child, Paul had been inquisitive about every aspect of his faith, never hesitating to ask whatever popped into his mind. "Why are the bitter herbs bitter?" the curious five-year-old asked his father. "Why is the Sabbath holey?" he asked his mother. "Is it old and worn out?"

Paul's childhood fascination with the Law grew. He mimicked his father's washing rites. While other boys were outside playing, he memorized the Jewish oral traditions. Judaism was his passion, so it wasn't a surprise when he left for Jerusalem to study to be a rabbi.

Paul's quick mind for the Law and traditions made him a favorite among the rabbis. Their encouragement fueled his zeal and he quickly advanced beyond his contemporaries. The Law was on his mind when he woke, ate, walked, talked, and went to bed. It dictated his every move. He had found his fulfillment in it, but something was still missing.

"Lord, now You are my life," Paul prayed. "Thank You for the joy I've found in You!"

◆ ◆ ◆

Mary scrubbed her father's and brothers' clothes. "What do they do all day?" she asked her mother. "Roll in the dirt?!" she complained. "When is a *nice* Christian going to come through Colossae and make me his bride?" Her mother smiled, thinking to herself, *And you won't be doing his wash?*

◆ ◆ ◆

Christ, Our Life

Reread Colossians 3:4.

1. Who is our life? ______

2. What do you think Paul means when he writes, "Christ, who is our life"?

______

______

______

As we might say about a child, "Volleyball is her life!" Or, about a doctor, "Medicine is his life." About a sports fanatic, "Sports is his life!" Or, a musician, "Music is her life." Paul writes, "Christ is our life."

Some of us might be thinking, *Well, I'm not as crazy about Jesus as Paul was. I love the Lord and am thankful He's saved me, but I can't honestly say He's my life. I'm not consumed with Him.*

The interesting thing is, Paul doesn't say, "When Christ, who is my life." He says, "our" life. I think he said that for several reasons. First, whether we acknowledge it or not, Christ truly is our life! No Christ, no life.

3. Look up the following Scriptures and record additional reasons why Christ truly is our life.

   Genesis 2:7 ______

   John 11:25 ______

   John 14:6 ______

   John 20:21–22 ______

   1 John 5:12–13 ______

Jesus not only gave us physical life, He gave us eternal life when He breathed His Holy Spirit into us. Your body can't live without breath. Your spirit can't live in heaven without the breath of the Holy Spirit in you. Your spirit breathes now and for eternity because of Christ! Christ *is* your life! Paul realized it and flourished in it. Many of us may not yet, but we can.

4. What are your thoughts concerning the fact that Christ is your life? ______________

____

5. What can you do if you haven't recognized Christ is your life?

   a) Get on your face and *apologize* to God.

   b) *Profess* (don't simply read) Galatians 2:20.

   c) Do what Romans 12:1 says. Get on your knees or bow your head. *Present* your body as a living sacrifice to God.

   d) Obey Romans 12:2. Begin diligently, prayerfully *studying* your Bible to transform your mind, in keeping with God's mind.

   e) Read 1 Corinthians 6:19–20. *Agree* with Jesus that you're not your own; you're His. Acknowledge that God bought you with Christ's blood. *Praise* Him for making you His temple, in whom His Holy Spirit dwells. Rejoice that God made you into a living and holy sanctuary through whom Christ can be magnified. What an honor!

   f) Read Ephesians 5:18. Confess and *repent* of anything that's filled—controlled—you in the past. *Ask* Jesus, who is your life, to fill and control you.

   g) Read 1 John 1:8–10. When you sin—which you will—*admit* it. Don't hide from or avoid God. Quickly pray. Stay in prayer and talk to God about what you did. Think through why you did it. Is it a habit, pattern, or stronghold? Was it a one-time occurrence or is it a red flag of something more going on inside of you? God can purify, cleanse, and create new habits in us when we sincerely and humbly go to Him. This process is called *sanctification*.

   h) Read Romans 12:4–8. *Recognize* that God has given you a spiritual gift and a place of service in the church. Filled with God's Spirit, attend and see how God prompts you to serve Him. Are you an encourager who tells the pastor the sermon was good? Then you may have the gift of encouragement. Do you highlight Scriptures and take notes? Then you may have the gift of knowledge or teaching. Do you have an idea for how something could be better organized? Then you probably have the gift of administration. Discover how the Lord wants to use you and then *serve* Him.

"Christ, who is our life!" Praise be to Him! One day, when you find He is your first thought and His passions drive your day, when you are consumed with Him, then join Paul and say, "Christ, who is our life!"

What is your prayer? ____

____

____

You Will Be Revealed with Christ in Glory

Reread Colossians 3:4.

7. In our study of Colossians 3:1–4, Paul contrasts two subjects. Record them below.

   Things above and ______________________________ (v. 2)

   Hidden and ______________________________ (vv. 3–4)

Paul is mindful we live in two spheres. He is awakening us to the spiritual.

8. We have studied in Colossians 3:4 that Christ is our life. Find two additional points in Colossians 3:4 and record them below.

   a) ______________________________

   b) ______________________________

In Colossians 3:4 Paul explains:
❑ Christ will be revealed in glory. ❑ We will be revealed in glory!

That which has been hidden—our life with Christ—is going to be revealed!

According to *The Exhaustive Concordance of the Bible*, *reveal* means "to make manifest or make actual and visible, realized." We look up at the heavens and know Christ is there, but we can't see Him. One day, we will. This divine revelation won't happen by us standing on earth and looking into the sky. Rather, we'll see Jesus when He appears in glory. The actual gathering of Christ's body in heaven will be realized! Hallelujah, praise the Lord! That's why Paul tells us to set our minds on the things above. What we do now for God's kingdom counts for eternity.

9. Paul writes more about Christ's and our future glory in 1 Corinthians 15:40–49. What thrills your soul as you read this passage? ____________________

10. Meditate on Philippians 3:20–21 and all Paul is telling you.

    Where is your citizenship? ____________________

    What is to be our state of mind in regard to Christ's coming? ____________________

What will Christ do in regard to your body? ____________________

____

____

____

What should we do in light of Christ's return? (1 John 3:3) ____________________

____

____

____

REREAD COLOSSIANS 3:1–4 WITH ALL WE'VE STUDIED IN MIND.
Are you in awe? Christ is coming back in glory. Since we're Christians, we should have our minds and affections on Him and heaven.

What's in Your Basket?

BASKET CASE

- My life is my job, children, sports.
- I forget about heaven and Jesus returning in glory.
- I think I'm losing my mind.

EXTRAORDINARY LIFE

- Christ is my life. I am consumed with Him as I carry out my daily responsibilities.
- I live in anticipation of Christ's glorious return.
- I keep my mind set on Christ above.

- ♦ *Perhaps I'm a basket case because I forget Christ is my life. I become too caught up in the world. I need to think more on Him.*
- ♦ *Perhaps I'm a basket case because I ignore the Bible teaching—to present my body to God.*
- ♦ *Perhaps I'm a basket case because I don't often confess my sins. I avoid discussing them with God. I blame others for my actions rather than own up to my sin before God.*
- ♦ *Perhaps I'm a basket case because I allow others to control me: my children, their commitments, my husband, work, temperament, food and drinking habits. I'm not Spirit-controlled.*
- ♦ *Perhaps I'm a basket case because I forget about heaven. I forget to live in light of seeing Jesus revealed in glory.*

Thinking It Over

♥ 1. What's on your heart in relation to "Christ, our life"?

♥ 2. What might God want you to do in light of what you've studied about Christ being our life?

♥ 3. What impressed you about being revealed with Christ in glory?

Weekly Wrap-Up

Where Am I? With which basket-case point do I most relate?

Where Do I Want to Be? To which aspects of extraordinary living is God calling me?

How Will I Get There? What golden nugget and/or verse do I want to remember to help me better address your basket-case moments and live an extraordinary life?

Thinking of Others: What from this week's study do I want to share with someone to encourage or warn them?

I pray you're filled with anticipation at the blessing and thought of Christ's returning in glory and you being revealed in glory with Him! Praise to our loving God!

◆ WEEK 6 ◆

WEARING YOUR WRONGS OR WEARING YOUR WINGS?

Glory—this is what God has for us and we don't have to wait until heaven to begin experiencing it. Paul invites us this week to put off our old self and go to "flight school" with Jesus.

◆ ◆ ◆

> Mary was perturbed with herself! She loved hearing Paul's letter and was enthusiastic about doing as he had written. However, she would often return home from church and do the exact opposite of that which would please the Lord. Disappointed, she knelt and asked for forgiveness. Later, when talking to her little brother, his wise comment surprised her: "At least you knew you messed up!" True, she was becoming more aware of how she could please the Lord. At least that was a step in the right direction.

◆ ◆ ◆

> Paul laid aside his dirty clothes as he climbed into bed. He had always held that cleanliness was next to holiness. However, the last few years hadn't allowed him to follow the ritual cleanliness to which he was accustomed. "Lord, thank You! Though my outer garments are dirty, my soul is clean because of You."

◆ ◆ ◆

DAY 1: *Put Aside the Old*

> Father, thank You for this day and the opportunity to serve You. Show me in today's study how I can lay aside my old self and walk in a manner worthy of You. In Jesus's name. Amen.

Paul is practical. He has laid a sound doctrinal foundation to teach us about Christ and all that He has accomplished on our behalf. He has warned us to guard against false teachings. He has encouraged us to hold fast to our faith. Now Paul begins connecting the dots between God's principles and our daily lives and decisions. He addresses the subject of our bodies, thoughts, emotions, morals, work ethic, and our relationships with spouses, children, bosses, and others.

READ COLOSSIANS 3:5–9.

1. What is the subject of verse 5?
   ❑ Our minds ❑ Our bodies

2. What does verse 5 tell us to do?
   ❑ Forget ❑ Consider

3. How does the Bible tell us to consider our bodies in relation to the things listed in verse 5?
   ❑ As alive ❑ As dead

4. Record five things to which we're to be dead.

   ____

   ____

   ____

   ____

   ____

Paul makes an interesting observation in Colossians 3:6. He says it's because of these sins that God's wrath is coming.

5. On whom is God's wrath coming?
   ❑ Sons of God ❑ Sons of disobedience

6. In verse 7, what clarification does Paul make, in case Christians might think God's wrath is coming on them?

____

____

LET'S CONSIDER THESE VERSES IN MORE DETAIL.

CONSIDER THE MEMBERS OF YOUR BODY AS DEAD

Consider the members of your earthly body as dead means "to put to death, slay, deprive of power." The verb tense of *consider* means "to commit to a decisive and effective choice. It's a command to "do this! Make this happen. (Don't just try.) Begin to do this now!" In other words, once and for all, make a decision not to do these things and stick with your decision.

William Barclay explains this passage means "put to death every part of your self which is against God and keeps you from fulfilling His will." Barclay quotes C. F. D. Moule:

> The Christian must kill self-centeredness and regard as dead all private desires and ambitions. There must be in his life a radical transformation of the will and a radical shift of the centre. Everything which would keep him from fully obeying God and fully surrendering to Christ must be surgically excised.

According to the *Ryrie Study Bible*, God is saying, "Put to death. Separate yourselves from the deeds of the old nature." Jesus expressed the same concept in Matthew 5:27–30 when He said to tear out your eye or cut off your hand if they cause you to stumble. By using a hyperbole (a giant exaggeration and overstatement), Jesus points to the seriousness of sin: sin leads to hell. Jesus has saved us from sin and hell. Now, we should stop practicing the sin He died to save us from.

7. Reread the list in Colossians 3:5. It is quite varied. Different "members" serve our body to carry out these sins. Beside each of the following sins, record the member of the body involved (arm, leg, mouth, heart, etc.). Definitions of the sins are listed following the words.

   Immorality ________________________________

   Impurity ________________________________

   Passion ________________________________

   Evil desire ________________________________

   Greed ________________________________

Immorality: "Illicit sexual intercourse; adultery, fornication, homosexuality, lesbianism, intercourse with animals, sexual intercourse with close relatives."

Impurity: "Uncleanness in a moral sense: the impurity of lustful, luxurious, profligate (reckless, wasteful, decadent) living; impure motives."

Passion: "A feeling that the mind suffers, depraved passion."

Evil desire: "Wrong, wicked, injurious, destructive, cravings." This describes a person who is driven by the desire for wrong things.

Greed: "Covetousness, a greedy desire to have more."

8. What does Paul say greed amounts to?
   ❑ No big deal ❑ Idolatry

Idolatry

Idolatry is the worship of false gods. Paul used the first part of his letter to address false teaching. Now he addresses false gods. These gods are persons or things that we treat as having supreme value and suppose control a particular aspect or part of reality.

False gods applies to things that control us, to which we give ourselves, around which our thoughts revolve, and on which we expend energy or money. Purchases don't end the desire for more. Money doesn't provide joy. Sex doesn't fill the hole in longing hearts.

9. How does Paul describe the relationship of believers to the above-mentioned sins?
   - ❑ They're walking and living in the sins
   - ❑ They once walked and lived in those sins

Walk

In Colossians 3:7, Paul acknowledges that the believers once walked in the sins he listed. However, as sons or daughters of God rather than children of disobedience, believers are called to a new life and walk (Colossians 1:10; 2:6).

Directives for Dying to Self

Paul gives two directives for dying to self—putting to death the habits of the old nature. We've already mentioned the first one: consider your body dead to those things.

First, Consider the Members of Your Body Dead to Sin

My mother and father are in heaven. Before death, they gave directives to physicians to not resuscitate them or keep them on life support. They considered beforehand what they wanted and their decisions were honored.

Our old nature has been crucified. God's directive to us is not to resuscitate sin. We need to follow through and give a directive to our body and mind that we're dead to sin and it's not to be resuscitated in our lives. Rather than keep the memory of sins alive, we're not to fuel our bodies or fan memories that resuscitate sins. We let them die because God tells us to do so.

10. Reread Colossians 3:8. What is the second directive?
    ❑ Put aside ❑ Put on

Second, Put Sin Aside

The second directive is to put sin aside. The visual is of taking off one's clothes. We're to strip old-nature sins from ourselves as if they're filthy, chemically toxic rags. We're not to wear them and thereby taint our souls and dishonor God.

11. List the sins that are improper clothing for our new nature. (Colossians 3:8)

______________________	______________________
______________________	______________________
______________________	lying (v.9)

Check the ones that find a way to the closet of your mind, emotions, or heart.

- ❑ *Anger*: "Temper, agitation of the soul, impulse, desire, any violent emotion."
- ❑ *Wrath*: "Anger forthwith boiling up and soon subsiding again."
- ❑ *Malice*: "Ill-will, desire to injure, wickedness, depravity, wickedness that's not ashamed to break laws."
- ❑ *Slander*: "Speech injurious to another's good name."
- ❑ *Abusive speech*: "Foul speaking, low and obscene speech."
- ❑ *Lying*: "To speak deliberate falsehoods, to deceive one by a lie."

What's in Your Basket?

Basket Case

- Consider my body alive to sin
- Put some sin aside, not all

Extraordinary Life

- Consider my body dead to sin
- Put all sin aside

- ♦ *Perhaps I'm a basket case because I haven't considered my body as dead to sin. I keep some sins alive by thinking about them and acting on them.*
- ♦ *Perhaps I'm a basket case because I haven't put certain sins aside. I still drag them out and wear them, although they're unbecoming to the Lord and my new nature.*

Thinking It Over

♥ 1. How serious is God about sin in you?

___

♥ 2. What points do you want to remember from today's study?

___

♥ 3. What verse would be good for you to remember?

___

DAY 2: *Put on the New Self*

Father, as Your Word convicts me, help me be quick to respond! Teach me how to live for You each moment of the day! In Jesus's name. Amen.

◆ ◆ ◆

Mary's eyes continued to open to the realization of how her faith differed from the Gnostics' beliefs. Her friend Rachel wasn't being taught about the sanctity of her body. Although the spiritist claimed enlightenment, she walked in darkness. Although she claimed spiritual freedom, she was a slave of her sin. In rejecting Christ, she turned her back on Christ's glorious upward calling.

◆ ◆ ◆

Epaphras was concerned about his flock in Colossae. He was grateful Paul was addressing sensitive issues with them. Many of the Colossian Christians were struggling. Some were pulled by their old lifestyles. Others were willing to live a godly life, but were married to unbelievers who didn't hold to godly values. Others admitted to struggling with their old nature, to lying, lust, greed, or anger.

Paul, Epaphras, and Timothy knelt and prayed for the believers to move beyond their cycle of sinning, repenting, and sinning again.

◆ ◆ ◆

READ COLOSSIANS 3:9–13.

1. What does Paul contrast in Colossians 3:9–10?
   - ❑ The old body and new body
   - ❑ The old self and new self

2. What does Colossians 3:10 say believers have put on? ______________________

____

____

Certainly we are inadequate to explain the profundity of all that God reveals. However, studying His truth is the means by which we grow and we experience Christ's power over sin in our lives.

PLEASE CONSIDER WHAT WE'VE STUDIED:

COLOSSIANS 1: Jesus is exalted as preeminent Lord over all rulers and authorities.

COLOSSIANS 2: Jesus substituted His life for ours on the Cross so we might die to sin and live to righteousness. We're identified with Jesus's death, burial, and resurrection.

Colossians 3: Jesus is ascended into heaven and we're identified with Christ in God. Our identity isn't on earth but in heaven. We're to set our minds on the things above. Christ has positioned us with Him, to reign eternally, beginning now with reigning over sin.

Because of who we are (new creations) and where we are (raised and seated with Christ), we're able to live victoriously in Christ. The means by which we're enabled is the Holy Spirit whom God gave us at salvation. His presence in our human spirits makes us spiritually alive, new creations. He's the empowering third person of the Godhead, with whom we're to be continuously filled so that Christ—not our flesh—rules over sin and glorifies God.

The written Word is strategic for us if we want to grow and overcome temptation. The Bible is the Living Word, which God uses to teach, convict, and train us in righteousness. The Holy Spirit enlightens our minds and prompts us to purity and growth on the basis of the knowledge and spiritual wisdom we acquire from the Bible.

3. Check the critical principle we're taught in Colossians 3:9–10.
   - ❑ As a Christian, I have both a new self and an old self.
   - ❑ As a Christian, I don't need to worry about how I live.

4. Write *True* or *False* beside the following statements. (Colossians 3:9–10)
   - ______________ I've already laid (put) aside the old self with its practices.
   - ______________ I've already put on the new self.
   - ______________ I haven't laid (put) aside the old self and practices.
   - ______________ I haven't put on the new self.

Laid or *put* expresses here "simple action, as opposed to continuous action." Believers have *already* put aside the old self and have *already* put on the new self. It occurred at salvation. However, if we want to experience Christ's power and dominion over sin, we must consider (reckon, count) our bodies as dead to sin.

Write Galatians 2:20, the key to living an extraordinary, victorious Christian life.

____

____

____

Notice, Paul doesn't say, "I'm going to try to crucify my old sin habits." That's incorrect theology. The old self is already laid aside... in the tomb, dead, and buried. My new self is a new creation God raised to walk in newness of life. It's stimulated by Christ's Spirit. In other words, Paul might say, "Observe my Christian works, but realize the source is Christ in me."

Let me repeat: The believer's old self is dead. If we skip this principle and attempt to live the Christian life, we'll fall flat on our faces. Until we come to a crisis of understanding, as Paul did (Romans 7:24) and comprehend that we are wretched and incapable of living the Christian life apart from Christ, we'll swim upstream in a river of despair (Romans 7:15). We must stop trying to swim against the current of our old nature in our own strength. We must stop flailing our arms and crying, "I'm not ever going to get past this." We must admit we can't live the Christian life. We must go limp in Christ's arms and let Him rescue us from the tidal waves of our old nature. By Christ's power we can turn from sin, swim out of our despair, and walk the shores of the victorious Christian life. The mystery, the secret to the Christian life, is Colossians 1:27.

5. Write out Colossians 1:27, prayerfully absorbing the mystery: Christ in you.

____

____

____

____

God willed to make known this mystery: Christ is in you. God isn't keeping Christ's presence in you a secret. But some of us aren't "getting it."

YOUR BODY = CHRIST'S HOME.

God wants to use our bodies and minds as the means to fulfill His purposes on earth. This is why it's critical for us to set our minds on the things above. He wants to use our minds for His heavenly purposes. He wants to use our bodies as His instruments. See why Colossians 3:5–9 is critical? Jesus doesn't want us to be used for ungodly purposes! Jesus wouldn't do those things and therefore we mustn't. When we sin, we're being offensive to Christ who lives in us. Bad behavior doesn't correctly represent Christ to those around us.

6. Our words, actions, and emotions are to be in keeping with whose image? (Colossians 3:10) ________________________________

____

7. Why does Jesus care how we think, act, and behave? What right does He have to tell us to live according to His image? Fill in the blank. (Colossians 3:10)

   He's my ____

Jesus is also the Creator of my new self. He has every right to dictate that I live in a way that glorifies Him.

YOU HAVE PUT ON THE NEW SELF

According to Colossians 3:10, our Creator has recreated us in Christ Jesus. We have put on a new self in Christ. We put on a "new, recently born" self. Our new self isn't our old self patched up or remodeled. This is important to understand. At salvation you were born anew (John 3:3–6). That's why Jesus explained to Nicodemus, "You must be born again." You must be born of God's Spirit or you're not going to heaven. Old-natured people who don't have God's Spirit are not in heaven. New Holy Spirit–natured people are in heaven. Have you been born anew by God's Spirit?

8. What does Colossians 3:10 tell believers about their "new" self?
   ❑ It's being renewed. ❑ It's being discarded.

Renewed

Our new self *is* being renewed. *Renew* means "to cause to grow up, to be given new strength and vigor." Isn't this wonderful news?

9. Peter speaks of believers as "newborn" babes, which is in keeping with Jesus's teaching that we must be born again. What does Peter tell us to do? (1 Peter 2:2)

____

____

Peter explains that, as newborn babies need milk in order to grow, so believers need the milk of God's Word to grow in respect to their salvation.

10. After sucking on the milk of the elementary principles of our faith, what's expected of believers? (1 Corinthians 3:1–2)
    ❑ Nurse on the milk of biblical principles.
    ❑ Chew the solid food of God's Word.

Christians mature by chewing on the meat of God's Word, as we're doing in this study. If we ignore the meat of God's Word regarding our old and new self, we'll be weak, baby Christians. If we chew on these teachings, we'll grow and mature. Christ is calling us to a victorious, extraordinary Christian walk.

What's in Your Basket?

Basket Case

- Old self thriving
- Drinking in the world
- Chewing on the world
- Spiritually stymied
- Weak and impotent to live Christian life

Extraordinary Life

- Old self dead—New self thriving
- Drinking in the Word
- Chewing on the Word
- Spiritually maturing
- Invigorated and empowered to live the Christian life

- *Perhaps I'm a basket case because I don't consider my old self as dead. I keep trying to patch up my old nature instead of close the casket lid on it.*
- *Perhaps I'm a basket case because I haven't been born again. I try to be good, but I've never turned to the Lord and received Christ and His eternal life. I'm not sure Christ's Spirit is in me.*
- *Perhaps I'm a basket case because I've been a Christian for a long time, but have never understood, or else have forgotten, that I've been crucified with Christ. I must consider myself dead to sin and ask Christ to live through me.*

Thinking It Over

♥ 1. How is God speaking to you? ____________________

♥ 2. If you've never committed your life to Christ, would you do so now? If you're a Christian, but need to recommit to being dead to sin and alive to Christ, won't you do so now? ____________________

♥ 3. What points and Scripture do you most want to remember from today's study?

Day 3: *Christ Is All and in All*

Father, forgive me when I judge people by the appearance of their eyes, the accent of their tongue, or their skin tone. Help me to see and to love others as You do. In Jesus's name. Amen.

Paul lay in bed pondering his dream and asking the Lord what, if anything, he was to learn from it. Not knowing whether his dream of a long lost friend was meaningless or if God was speaking to him, Paul took his dream to the Lord. In God's presence, Paul considered the lost friendship; lost because of Paul's faith in Christ and his friend's denouncement of Christ. As Paul recalled the final blow to their friendship, God interrupted Paul's thoughts and turned his mind to the present. Paul couldn't change the past, but he could learn from it. With resolve to not listen to Satan's accusations of already forgiven sins, Paul pressed forward.

◆ ◆ ◆

Mary, who was a saver, kept everything she got her hands on. Pots or pieces of fabric that others discarded, she kept. Perhaps that's why her mind rejoiced that God *saved* her. God considered her worthy of saving although others might toss her aside. She might not be of worth to others, but her worth to Jesus meant everything.

◆ ◆ ◆

No Distinction

Reread Colossians 3:9–11.

1. Paul speaks of renewal in verses 10 and 11. Record the definition for renew given earlier this week.

____

____

2. How does Colossians 3:11 tell us to view people of different nationalities, appearances, etc.? Check one.
   ❑ As distinct ❑ As not being distinct

3. Fill in the following blanks in which Paul identifies different people groups.

   Greek and _______________

   Circumcised and _______________

   Barbarian and _______________

   Slave and _______________

The above groups may not be people of whom we're often mindful. It's probably been a while since we've run into a barbarian. Though the different people listed may not stand out to us, in Paul's day the people listed wouldn't have considered mingling with one another. Paul's words in Colossians 3:11 were revolutionary. Unfortunately, even in our day, prejudicial thinking and behavior exists. Therefore these Scriptures are applicable. In them we see that God holds no distinction among His people.

4. Check the following barriers, which Christ erased.
   ❑ Birth and nationality ❑ Religious ceremony and ritual
   ❑ Cultural ❑ Economic
   ❑ Political ❑ Academic

5. What additional barrier does Galatians 3:28 point out that Christ removed?

____

____

6. What point does Paul make in Galatians 3:28 that affirms his point in Colossians 3:11? ____________________

____

____

7. READ GALATIANS 3:26. How does God consider all who have come to faith in Christ? ______________________________

____

____

8. READ EPHESIANS 2:12–13. Lest any of us are prideful, what should we remember?

____

____

Definitions List

- *Greeks* were the aristocrats of the ancient world. To them, anyone who didn't speak Greek was a barbarian.
- *Jews* looked down on all other nations, regarding them as unclean, uncircumcised.
- *Scythians* were inhabitants of Scythia, or a section of modern-day Russia, and were regarded as the wildest of barbarians. Scythian equaled "rude or rough."
- *Slaves* weren't even classified in ancient law as human beings. There could be no serious fellowship between slaves and those who were free.
- *Women* had virtually no rights and were often regarded as property.

9. It's easy to skim through Colossians 3:10. However, would you agree or disagree there are still prejudices in our day?
   ❑ Agree ❑ Disagree

10. Check any of the following if it is a barrier still seen in society.
   ❑ Religious ❑ Intellectual
   ❑ Social ❑ Cultural
   ❑ Other: ❑ Economic ____________________

11. What should your position be regarding believers who are culturally, socially, or academically different from you? ____________________

____

____

12. Just between you and God, what *is* your view of people, even believers, who are different from you? ____________________

____

____

13. Think and pray about God's Word. Pray for yourself and others to be obedient to Christ's calling regarding Colossians 3:11.

14. What can you do to help remove prejudices and false distinctions? ____________________

____

____

15. Reread Colossians 3:11. What or who unites various people? ____________________

____

____

Christ Is All and in All

We've already studied how all the fullness of God is in Jesus. We've also studied how Jesus is *in* Christians (Colossians 1:27). Christ permeates not only heaven, but also our spirits through His Spirit. I can't help but wonder when Paul wrote Colossians 3:11 if he was thinking of Pentecost, when God sent the promised Holy Spirit and birthed the New Testament church. Acts 2:2–11 recounts people of all nations miraculously hearing the gospel in their own languages. The promise for Jews was expanded to all people. That for which Jesus prayed, that He be *in* Christians, was fulfilled (John 17:23). God sent the Holy Spirit, for whom Jesus told the disciples to wait (Acts 1:4–5). Believers of all nationalities, classes, and cultures were baptized into one body. Wouldn't that have been a glorious day to witness?

16. What resulted from the believers' repentance, salvation, and baptism in the Holy Spirit? (Acts 2:41–47) ____________________

____

____

____

At the Tower of Babel, God separated people into nations with different languages (Genesis 11:1, 9). At Pentecost, God reunites believers of all nations and languages in one body in Christ. In heaven, we'll all worship at Christ's feet (Revelation 5:9–10). Praise be to Him!

What's in Your Basket?

Basket Case

- Look at people's external trappings
- Select relationships on the basis of cultural differences

Extraordinary Life

- Look at Christ in others
- Fellowship with all God's children

♦ *Perhaps I'm a basket case because I put up social, economic, academic, or other barriers; all of which Christ removed.*

♦ *Perhaps I'm a basket case because I don't look for Christ in others. I'm absorbed with external trappings rather than Christ in people.*

Thinking It Over

♥ 1. To what degree do you think national, cultural, and economic barriers exist among believers?

♥ 2. What are you doing to model unity among diverse believers?

♥ 3. What Scripture or nugget of truth do you want to remember from today's study?

Day 4: *Put on God's Heart*

Father, thank You for this day and the opportunity to study Your Word. Help me apply each truth to my heart. In Jesus's name. Amen.

Mary woke thinking about the difference between her old self and new self. Listening to Paul's explanation of who she was in Jesus gave her hope. "Lord Jesus, fill me with Your thoughts and attitudes today. Help me honor and love others in whom You dwell." With a smile on her face, she headed out the door. Finally she understood the struggles she'd been experiencing weren't against others. She'd been battling her thoughts and feelings. *How have I let this go for so long?* she wondered. *When did I begin being so negative?*

◆ ◆ ◆

The guard assigned to Paul scrutinized God's humble servant. Finally, he asked, "Paul, what makes you tick? How do you continue to be kind and patient in the midst of your imprisonment?"

◆ ◆ ◆

Read Colossians 3:12–14.

Do you ever forget who you are and whose you are? Coaches don't let their players forget. They remind them, "We're the fighting Tigers!" In other words, "Go out there and fight to get that ball! Fight to win! You're a mean, tough Tiger!" Nations also remind citizens who they are. We fly flags and sing national anthems. Parents may call children to proper behavior by saying, "Act like a Jones," or whatever the family name is. In Colossians 3:12 and following, Paul reminds us to whom we belong. He calls us to reflect God's ways in our thoughts, attitudes, and relationships with one another.

1. In what three ways does Paul describe believers? (Colossians 3:12) ____________

____

____

Chosen, Holy, Beloved

"Chosen of God, holy, beloved" should be laminated and worn daily as a reminder of who we Christians are. Would it make a difference if it were dangling as a necklace from your neck as you disciplined your children? Would it cause you to think twice before you honked your horn at someone who edged into your parking place? How would the reminder affect you when you're grappling with feelings of low self-worth? What effect would the reminder have on Satan as he prowls, seeking someone to devour? Might he turn and look for someone weak in his or her faith, rather than you? How might "chosen, holy, and beloved" affect the tone of your voice when meeting with a coach, teacher, or business associate with whom you're frustrated? How would it affect your attitude toward your spouse, sibling, or parent?

2. Write Ephesians 1:4, a verse similar to Colossians 1:12, in the first person.

____

____

God chose (elected) us to be holy and blameless. He loves us. Since we weren't holy and blameless, He made us holy and blameless in Christ. Now, God wants us to act like who we are and whose we are.

3. In order to act like we are His, what does God tell us to do?
   ❑ Take off the extra pounds. ❑ Put on a certain kind of heart.

4. Why does God tell us to put on a certain kind of heart? (Matthew 12:34)

____

____

5. In addition to the mouth speaking good things from what fills the heart, what else can flow from hearts? (Matthew 15:19) ______________________________

____

____

Our words and actions come from that which fills our hearts! Therefore our hearts are important to God. Our hearts are key if we want to reflect Christ.

According to *The Exhaustive Concordance of the* Bible, *heart* in the Bible referred to the "bowels or intestines. The bowels were regarded as the seat of the more violent passions, such as anger and love; but they were viewed by the Hebrews as the seat of the tenderer affections, especially kindness, benevolence, compassion."

6. Does God care about our hearts? Absolutely! What did the psalmist know that we do well to know? (Psalm 66:18) ______________________________

____

____

The psalmist recognized that if he held things in his heart that weren't good, his fellowship with God would be negatively affected. Do we recognize that? Are we aware God weighs the attitude and actions of our hearts? (Proverbs 21:2) Could it be we suffer unanswered prayer and lack of direction because we have a "heart" condition?

Today we can have a checkup with our Great Physician and renowned cardiologist. Use the following to check how healthy your heart is.

7. List indications of a spiritually healthy heart. (Colossians 3:12–14)

   Verse 12 ____

   Verse 12 ____

   Verse 12 ____

   Verse 12 ____

Verse 12 ____

Verse 13 ____

Verse 13 ____

Verse 14 ____

Continue your heart checkup by checking any of the following you've experienced in the last 12 months. Be honest, since God can clearly see your heart. Place a check in the box to show how often.

Unmerciful toward others	❑ Never	❑ Seldom	❑ Frequently	❑ Often
Unkind	❑ Never	❑ Seldom	❑ Frequently	❑ Often
Prideful.	❑ Never	❑ Seldom	❑ Frequently	❑ Often
Lack tenderness toward others	❑ Never	❑ Seldom	❑ Frequently	❑ Often
Impatient	❑ Never	❑ Seldom	❑ Frequently	❑ Often
Low ability to endure with others	❑ Never	❑ Seldom	❑ Frequently	❑ Often
Difficulty forgiving	❑ Never	❑ Seldom	❑ Frequently	❑ Often
Lack of love	❑ Never	❑ Seldom	❑ Frequently	❑ Often

There's a solution if you're suffering from one of the above heart problems. What's our Great Physician's remedy? Put on Christ's heart (Colossians 3:12). *Put on* means "sink into (clothing), clothe yourself," with Christ's compassion, kindness, humility, gentleness, patience, forbearance, forgiveness, and love.

How important is it for us to put on compassion, kindness, humility, gentleness, patience; to bear with one another; forgive as the Lord has forgiven us; and put on love? Very! We need to be vessels of God's compassion. An unruly child starving for attention needs our compassion. A family member or neighbor going through a difficult time needs our compassion.

Likewise, we are to be kind people. Throughout Scripture, God is praised for His loving-kindness. We can attend Bible studies and know all the right things to do; but if we're not kind, we're self-righteous robots.

Humility is one of the greatest Christian virtues and stands in stark contrast to pride and arrogance. Humility isn't cringing submission or thinking poorly of ourselves. Rather, it's humble submission to God and service toward others.

Gentleness isn't weakness. It's power under control. It's kindness and strength exercised under Christ's control. It's a mother firmly, lovingly disciplining her children rather than lashing out. It's a wife boldly speaking the truth in love to her husband rather than being cutting or rude to him.

To be patient and bear with one another means to be long-tempered rather than short-tempered. It's holding up when under pressure. We may tire of situations or even people. However, as Christ bears with us, we're to bear with others.

Finally, we're to forgive others. How can we withhold forgiveness when Christ forgave us?

What's in Your Basket?

Basket Case

- Coldhearted
- Unkind
- Prideful
- Hard
- Impatient
- Quit on others
- Unforgiving
- Unloving

Extraordinary Life

- Compassionate
- Kind
- Humble
- Gentle
- Patient
- Bear with others
- Forgiving
- Loving

♦ *Perhaps I'm a basket case because I don't put on Christ's heart of compassion, kindness, humility, gentleness, patience, and love.*

♦ *Perhaps I'm a basket case because I don't bear with others as Christ bears with me. I'm demanding and want everyone to shape up—yesterday!*

♦ *Perhaps I'm a basket case because I withhold forgiveness. I'm tied up in knots of blame, anger, and resentment.*

Thinking It Over

♥ 1. Look back over today's lesson. How would God sum up the condition of your heart? ____

♥ 2. In what area is there a lack of Christ's heart? In which area is the Holy Spirit not flowing? Would you repent and confess that before the Lord? Verse 13

♥ 3. Prayerfully ask the Lord to cleanse you so His Spirit can flow through you. Prayerfully put on Christ's heart.

♥ 4. Which verse do you want to remember or memorize? Why? ________________

____

____

____

Day 5: *Forgiveness, Love, Peace*

Father, in the midst of hectic days, I often forget to clothe myself in Your love. Too often I withhold forgiveness. Too often I don't let Your peace rule my heart. Forgive me. Work in me today so I reflect Your love, forgiveness, and peace. In Jesus's name. Amen.

♦ ♦ ♦

Paul had done things "right" all of his life. As a Hebrew of Hebrews and Pharisee, he'd lived by the Law. But love and peace? Compassion and kindness? Humility and gentleness? Forgiveness and bearing with one another? Those words didn't necessarily describe Paul before his salvation. Visiting with his guard, he explained the profound difference Christ made in his life. "You can do everything according to the rules. But if you don't love and forgive others, how much peace and joy can you have in your life?"

♦ ♦ ♦

"God wants us to experience Christ's love, forgiveness, and peace," Onesimus explained to Mary.

"I know the Lord Jesus loves and forgives me," Mary responded to Onesimus.

"Yes, Mary, but what Paul is talking about is us experiencing His love and peace in our hearts toward others. He wants us to forgive as He has forgiven us."

♦ ♦ ♦

Today we're going to continue discovering qualities that are ours in Christ. God has provided a divine wardrobe with which we're to clothe ourselves. Daily we're to put off anxious thoughts or an unforgiving spirit. Daily we're to put on Christ's love, forgiveness, and peace. Isn't it time we had a radical makeover?

Read Colossians 3:12–17.

1. What does Colossians 3:12 tell us to put on? (Try writing it from memory.)

____

____

____

2. In addition to putting on compassion, kindness, humility, gentleness, and patience, what does Colossians 3:13 tell us to do? ______________________________

____

____

____

Bear with and Forgive One Another

In today's society there's a serious absence of bearing with and forgiving one another.

Our tolerance for evil is growing, but our tolerance for one another isn't. Bearing with one another means "to hold up, to sustain, to endure." The opposite is to quit on each other, to not hold up, to not keep going, to not endure. Bearing with one another affects every relationship of our lives: spousal, parental, sibling, extended family, church relationships, work relationships, community and school relationships.

Whether you're in a difficult marriage; in the throes of child rearing toddlers, tweens, teens; serving as the caregiver to aging parents; or battling your own nightmares, sins, or addictions, God has a word for you: Don't give up. Hang in there! A favorite Scripture offers hope and encouragement: Luke 1:37.

3. Write Luke 1:37 in the following space or perhaps on a note card and place it where you can see it and be reminded of it. Perhaps hide it in your heart so you can carry it with you wherever you go. ______________________________

____

____

____

With God, Nothing Is Impossible

In our day, when it's easy to find escape in food, drink, pills, moving out, or changing jobs, God encourages us to bear with one another.

4. What is a key to bearing with one another? (Colossians 3:13)

❑ Having a shopping mall close by ❑ Chips
❑ Chocolate ❑ Forgiving one another

Some of us may try to eat, drink, or shop ourselves into endurance. However, Colossians 3:13 states that forgiveness is *key*. *Forgive* means "to show one's self gracious, kind, benevolent, to pardon freely, to grant forgiveness, graciously to restore one to another." Aren't we glad God forgave us and graciously, freely restored us to Himself?

5. What does Paul remind us in regard to those with whom we have a complaint?

____

____

Ouch! There's no wiggling out of that verse. Paul reminds us that just as God forgave us, we are to forgive rather than hold to our complaints, anger, and unforgiveness.

6. What does God's Word tell you about forgiving the person whom you've not yet forgiven?
   ❑ You should forgive. ❑ You shouldn't forgive.

We may need to underline the words *you should* in our Bibles as a reminder. There is no escape clause in this passage. There's no court of God in which He says, "Let me hear your case. What they did to you was so bad, you shouldn't forgive them." Would we like to stand before God and be judged in that manner? It makes me nervous thinking about it. No, we want God to forgive us no matter how badly we've behaved. God wants us to turn and exercise the same forgiveness.

Does forgiving someone mean what they did was OK? No. Does forgiving someone mean you have to put yourself in harm's way with the person again? No. Does forgiving mean the person won't be judged or pay for what he or she did? The blessing is, we don't have to figure that out! The person will stand before God. Vengeance is His. He will repay (Hebrews 10:30). Our responsibility is to obey God and forgive as He instructs us.

7. Do you have a complaint against someone? Why not relieve yourself of the anger and grant forgiveness? You can't be responsible for how the person responds, but you can take control of your responsibility before God. What is your response to God's Word? Will you trust, obey, and forgive? ______________________________

____

____

____

♦ *Perhaps I'm a basket case because God's told me to forgive and I'm rebelling against Him.*

Beyond All . . . Put On Love

Reread Colossians 3:14.

8. What does Paul say to do beyond all else? ______________________________

____

"Put on love." It's interesting that commentators explain Paul's use of *beyond all* is best translated "upon." In other words, if you're layering your virtuous clothes of compassion, kindness, humility, gentleness, patience, long-suffering, and forgiveness, remember to put love as your top outer garment.

9. How does Paul describe love in Colossians 3:14? ______________________________

____

____

Love is the belt that holds everything else together. It's the jacket, the outer garment, that must be seen. As Wuest words Colossians 3:14, "And upon all these, put on divine love which is a binding factor of completeness." Have you ever had a great outfit, but it lacked something? Perhaps a belt, earrings, the right shoes, jacket, or necklace? Love is the complement to all the other divine virtues. Don't leave home without it!

Without love, what do we look and sound like? A shiny, polished, clanging cymbal who annoys others (1 Corinthians 13).

♦ *Perhaps I'm a basket case because I rush out the door without Christ's love permeating every fiber of my being.*

Peace

Reread Colossians 3:15.

10. Have you ever been like Mary in our previous story? You know God established peace with you through Christ. However, as moment by moment goes by, peace eludes you?
❑ Yes ❑ No

11. Whose peace does Paul say we can experience? ______________________________

____

Paul makes a great observation in this verse. We need Christ's peace, not only as a state of our salvation, but also His peace flowing through our hearts. How is it possible to have Christ's peace? The same way we experience God's other virtues. When Christ established our peace with God, a conduit of grace opened to us.

The Holy Spirit freely flows from heaven into our spirits. The virtues Paul tells us to put on are not mere human virtues; they are godly virtues. Our capacity to wear them is divinely given. As a friend might give you her clothes to wear, God gives us His divine character to wear. You pick up His character in your spiritual closet, where the Holy Spirit has racks of love, compassion, kindness, humility, long-suffering, forgiveness, and gentleness. As a matter of fact, the Holy Spirit gives you the coat of His divinely colored qualities right off His back. "Here, take it! Put all these on! *Please... take it*," He urges us. "Take off your rags of bitterness, worry, unkindness. Put on my coat of divine qualities."

Peace means the "tranquil state of a soul assured of its salvation through Christ, and so fearing nothing from God and content with its earthly lot, of whatsoever sort that is." Peace is what Jesus left us, the peace that's out of this world! (John 14:27) It's the peace

God gave me when Taylor was two and I was diagnosed with ovarian cancer. It's the peace God wants you to experience.

12. What does Colossians 3:15 tell us to let peace do? ______________________________

____

I love these verses, don't you?

Rule means to be an umpire, decide, determine, direct, control. Wuest quotes Lightfoot on this passage, "Wherever there is a conflict of motives or impulses or reasons, the peace of Christ must step in and decide which is to prevail." Wuest quotes Vincent, "The previous reference to occasions for meekness, long-suffering, forbearance, forgiveness, etc., indicates a conflict of passions and motives in the heart. Christ is the one who adjusts all these, so that the metaphorical sense is appropriate."

When you're experiencing Christ's peace, a traffic jam doesn't throw you for a loop because you know God can make all things work together for good. Peace is not going crazy when well-laid plans fall apart because you know God has a better plan. You prayerfully turn your situation over to Him and let Him rule. Peace is knowing that God can work in your child's life even when things look grim. Peace is letting Christ calm raging storms that threaten to blow you off course. Peace is trusting your marriage to God as you let Him rule over your emotions, mind, and actions. Peace is not fearing the unknown, but rather resting in God who knows all.

♦ *Perhaps I'm a basket case because I don't allow God's peace to flow in and through me. I'm uptight, worrisome, and controlling instead of praying and resting in His divine peace.*

What's in Your Basket?

Basket Case

- I'm not about to forgive the one who wronged me.
- Love probably isn't the first thing someone notices about me.
- I don't know the last time I experienced true peace.

Extraordinary Life

- I've chosen to forgive as Christ forgave me.
- I ask God daily to fill me with His love.
- I praise God for Christ's peace.

♦ *Perhaps I'm a basket case because I know I should forgive, but I refuse to obey God. I'm angry and miserable.*

♦ *Perhaps I'm a basket case because I rush out the door without God's love clothing my heart.*

- *Perhaps I'm a basket case because I worry all the time. I wrap my mind around whatever is bothering me instead of opening my heart to be filled with Christ's peace.*

Thinking It Over

♥ 1. What's on your heart regarding

Forgiveness? ____________________

____

____

____

Love? ____________________

____

____

____

Peace? ____________________

____

____

____

♥ 2. What do you think God wants you to do in light of today's study?

____

____

____

♥ 3. What verse do you most need to memorize? Why? ____________________

____

____

____

♥ 4. If there's someone you need to forgive, won't you do so today? If there's someone with whom you've withheld love, would you humbly make amends?

____

____

____

God's greatest blessings flow through those who are willing not simply to study about Him, but to act on what they learn. I pray you're blessed, sister, as you ask Christ to fill and clothe you with His holy virtues.

Weekly Wrap-Up

Where Am I? With which basket-case point do I most relate?

____

____

____

Where Do I Want to Be? To which aspects of extraordinary living is God calling me?

____

____

____

How Will I Get There? What golden nugget and/or verse do I want to remember to help me better handle my basket-case moments and live an extraordinary life?

____

____

____

Thinking of Others: What from this week's study do I want to share with someone to encourage or warn them?

____

____

____

◆ WEEK 7 ◆

ARE YOU KIDDING?

Our study this week begins with a biblical look at relationships. As believers, we have a higher calling than the world. We have the blessed privilege of trusting God's ways are the right ways. Though the world may say, "Are you kidding?" our lives can reflect the extraordinary God we serve.

◆ ◆ ◆

If you had asked Mary, she would have told you how much she loved her family. However, one thing bothered Mary increasingly. At first, she hadn't been able to put her finger on it. However, as she meditated on Paul's letter, it finally occurred to her what it was. Her mother didn't sing like she had when she first became a Christian. Mary had loved hearing her sing psalms and praises as she cooked or did the dishes. As she reflected on those earlier years, she thought of what now filled their home. Rather than songs of praise, it was words of complaint. The weather was bad. The elder talked too long. The deacons were planning a project that would never work. They didn't have enough money. Taxes were too high. Her aches and pains were a constant source of disgruntlement. Even when their family took a day off to go to Hierapolis to enjoy the healing springs, her mother found something about which to complain. The lines were too long, the waters too hot or not hot enough. "What happened, Mama? Why do you complain so much? Why do you not sing?" Mary longed to ask, but didn't dare.

◆ ◆ ◆

Paul woke shivering from the cold. His threadbare cover hardly kept him warm. "Thank You, Lord, for this day. Thank You for the roof over my head. Thank You for the visitors You'll bring my way and with whom I can share about Christ. Thank You for being ever present, for being the Guardian of my soul. Keep my mind set on You today so I bring glory to Your name. Amen."

◆ ◆ ◆

DAY 1: *Let the Word of God Richly Dwell Within You*

Father, thank You for your love, mercy, and forgiveness. Thank You for giving me Your Word so I can learn and grow. Penetrate my mind and heart today with Your truths so I can live an extraordinary life that brings You glory. In Jesus's name. Amen.

Whether you're single, married, or widowed; whether you are a parent or have parents living; and whether you have children or have spiritual children, God's teachings will bless you.

Read Colossians 2:12–15.

1. As you think about your various relationships, which of the virtues in Colossians 3:12–15 do you most need to put on? For instance, do you need compassion toward a child or patience with a co-worker? List your relationships and the virtues you need to put on with each.

Relationship	Virtue I Need to Put On
__________	__________
__________	__________
__________	__________
__________	__________
__________	__________

2. As you think about your relationships, is there anyone God is calling you to "bear with"? (Colossians 3:13)
   ❑ Yes ❑ No

3. Is there anyone you need to forgive, although that person is in debt to you because of his or her sin? (Colossians 3:13) (See also Matthew 18:21–35.)
   ❑ Yes ❑ No

4. How well are you obeying God's command to put on love? Before you answer, consider His definition of love in 1 Corinthians 13. __________

____

____

____

5. What *rules* your heart and mind? Christ's peace or worries? (Colossians 3:15)

____

____

____

6. How might your relationships be different if you allowed the peace of Christ to "rule" your heart? Seriously think about this. ______________________

____

____

7. If you were to focus on what you're thankful for rather than what you may not like about your children, spouse, friends, co-workers, church members, or others, how might this affect your relationships? (Colossians 3:15) ______________________

____

____

8. Read Colossians 3:16. What are you to let dwell within you?
   ❑ Worry ❑ Word of Christ

9. What word describes how Christ's Word is to dwell within us?
   ❑ Randomly ❑ Richly

Notice, Paul's inspired letter tells us to let God's Word *richly dwell* within us. We can remind ourselves of this by simply saying that aloud: "I am to let God's Word *richly dwell* within me." That means everything we've studied up to this point is to be alive in us, affecting our lives. Paul, in effect, warns us, "Don't just read through this letter. Don't skim over virtues you're to put on. Don't try to wiggle off the spiritual hook by saying, 'Well, you don't know my husband.' Or, 'If you had my children . . .'"

The fact is, Christians experience problems, trials, and temptations like everyone else. It is our responses to problems, trials, and temptations that set us apart from unbelievers. Problems, trials, and temptations provide the forum through which we can demonstrate Christ's extraordinary life in us! When we're confronted with situations that can provoke responses that are not Christlike, we clash at the intersection of our flesh and the Spirit. This is the JOY crisis—Jesus Over You! We are to let Jesus Christ, who is in us, rule. Do things His way. Move over. Yield to Christ. Let Him reign in our hearts and minds. Trust God's way is best. Trust Him.

10. Reread Colossians 3:16. Who might notice if you were a singing mama or complaining mama, a cheerful wife or contentious wife, a thankful employee or grumbling employee, a cranky caregiver or cheerful caregiver? Circle which better describes you in the above relationships.

11. What insight does Jesus give on the subject of what comes out of our mouths? (Luke 6:45) ______________________

____

____

The Lord Jesus says our mouths are spigots for our hearts. What comes from our mouths is what fills our hearts. We can fill our hearts with Christ's treasures of compassion, forgiveness, and peace or we can fill our hearts with grumbling, narrow-minded complaints, unrealistic expectations of others, and general discontent. If we want to know what's in our hearts, we don't need an x-ray. We can listen to ourselves.

12. What is supposed to fill and flow from believers' hearts and mouths? (Colossians 3:16) ____

13. In what manner are we to relate to one another? (Colossians 3:16)

Regardless of our stage in life, we have the opportunity and God-blessed calling to teach and encourage others God's Word. Paul's admonition reminds us of Moses's words in Deuteronomy 6:5–7.

> "*You shall love the* LORD *your God with all your heart and with all your soul and with all your might. These words, which I am commanding you today, shall be on your heart. You shall teach them diligently to your* [*children*] *and shall talk of them when you sit in your house and when you walk by the way and when you lie down and when you rise up.*"

When God's Word richly dwells in our hearts, we have godly, encouraging words for a child who comes home from school with a backpack of troubles. We have godly, encouraging words for a short-tempered co-worker. We have wise, encouraging responses for a disgruntled spouse. Spiritual responses are different from fleshly reactions.

When discouragement or anger rises up, we can practice Jesus's way over our way. Matthew 26:30 states that Jesus, after confronting Judas who was betraying Him, sang a hymn and went with His disciples to the Mount of Olives. If Jesus sang a hymn and the Bible tells us to sing hymns and psalms, let's try it the next time we're down, discouraged, tempted, betrayed, or facing a trial.

What's in Your Basket?

Basket Case

- The Word of Christ is in my Bible on the shelf.
- I sing pity party songs.
- My mouth is a spigot for worldly thoughts that fill my heart.

Extraordinary Life

- The Word of Christ richly dwells in me.
- I enjoy singing praises and hymns to Jesus.
- Christ's words and thoughts flow out of my mouth from my heart.

♦ *Perhaps I'm a basket case because Christ's Word doesn't dwell in me.*

♦ *Perhaps I'm a basket case because I don't practice JOY. I do things my way instead of God's.*

♦ *Perhaps I'm a basket case because I sing pity party songs. Maybe I should practice singing hymns and praises to Jesus.*

Thinking It Over

♥ 1. How serious do you think Christ is about His words ruling your heart? Why do you think Christ wants His words, rather than your fleshly worries or reactions, to rule your heart? ________________________________

____

♥ 2. What songs, hymns, and spiritual songs do you like to sing when you're discouraged, tired, or unhappy? What songs do you like to sing when you're happy and rejoicing?

Discouraged: ____________________________________

Happy: ____

♥ 3. What golden nugget do you want to remember from today's study?

____

____

Day 2: *Biblical Principles for Marriage*

Father, Thank You for the richness of Your Word that teaches me everything I need for life. Thank You for loving me and positioning me in Christ as an heir of salvation. In Jesus's name. Amen.

♦ ♦ ♦

Mary's dream was to marry a kind Christian man, so she prayed daily for such a spouse. Her father was a good man, but he hadn't always been kind to her mother. However, since he had become a Christian, Mary had seen a drastic change in her father. "Thank You, Lord," she whispered as she laid her head on her pillow and drifted to sleep.

◆ ◆ ◆

Paul lay in bed and thought about all the people who'd visited him the past week. "Thank You, Lord," he prayed as he thought of the three legalistic Jews to whom he had explained grace. Next, his thoughts leaped to the Roman soldier who converted to Christianity. It had been a joy when Paul finally helped him understand the importance of standing firm in the midst of spiritual battles as he did in earthly battles. His thoughts wandered next to a Christian woman who finally understood she could put on Christ's virtues even as she put on her clothes. His last visitors, a Christian couple with seven children, lingered on his mind. They wanted to abide by their newfound faith, but when it was all said and done, were unhappy in their marriage. The pressures of the world, the sin tendencies each brought into the relationship, his meager paying job, and her weariness at raising seven children was taking a toll on their marriage. Their love for one another had turned to bitterness years before they had come to know Christ.

◆ ◆ ◆

With each day's study, Paul hits closer and closer to where we live. Whether you're single, divorced, happily or unhappily married, or a widow, please join me in looking with new eyes at God's Word. Read the Scriptures not only for yourself, but also with others in mind, whom you may have the opportunity to encourage one day.

Foundational Principles

As we look at biblical principles concerning marriage, we'll refer both to Colossians and Ephesians quite a bit, so you may want to bookmark them. Let's first read Colossians 3:18–19, Ephesians 5:18–25, and 2 Corinthians 6:14–15.

Marriage Principle 1

1. What is the first biblical principle of marriage? (2 Corinthians 6:14–15)
   - ❑ Christians should marry whoever they want, Christian or non-Christian.
   - ❑ Christians are to marry Christians.

Marriage Principle 2

2. What is a second biblical principle for marriage? (Ephesians 5:18, 21)
   - ❑ Husbands and wives, filled with the Spirit, are to be subject to one another in the fear of Christ.
   - ❑ Husbands and wives who have little regard for Christ and one another should expect to have successful marriages.

3. If you're married to an unbeliever (or someone who says he's a Christian, but doesn't bear any evidence of being a Christian), you should: (1 Corinthians 7:13)
   ❑ Leave him. ❑ Stay with him.

4. Why would a Christian stay with an unbelieving spouse? (1 Corinthians 7:14)

____

____

Our third principle is to stay with an unbelieving husband with the prayer that the unbeliever will come to salvation. A Christian wife's presence in the home is Jesus's presence in the home. It provides an opportunity for her husband and children to see Jesus. If you are married to an unbeliever, you have a missions field under your own roof. You don't have to fly to a faraway nation to serve Christ. Rather, each day, you have the opportunity to witness. You crawl in bed with your missions field. You feed your missions field. One day, the hope is, your spouse will be ripe for harvest and will be saved (Matthew 9:36–38). That's what happened with my mama and daddy.

Mama assumed Daddy was a Christian when they married because he was a member of a church and a nice man. However, he wasn't a Christian. Eventually, their marriage suffered. Mama raised my two sisters and me in church. One day, Daddy realized he was losing his family. Daddy turned to the Lord. After being saved, he became a great man of God who eagerly shared his faith in Jesus with others. The same can happen with your unbelieving husband. Never give up! With God all things are possible! (Luke 1:37)

Following are tips to help you take care of yourself, whether you're in a stressful or good marriage. If you're not married, the principles can be applied to any relationship.

✔ Meditate on the words of the Bible. Our behavior flows from our thoughts. Renew your mind each day in God's Word. Examine your thoughts in light of God's teachings.

✔ Look up, *heavenward*, and P.R.A.Y. When Peter kept His eyes on Jesus he was able to walk on water. When he took his eyes off Jesus, he began to sink. *Praise* God each day for who He is and for His blessings. *Repent* of your sins. *Ask* Jesus for your needs. *Yield* to God's voice as He directs you through your day (from *Pray with Purpose, Live with Passion*).

✔ Demonstrate what it means to be filled with the Spirit. Practice patience rather than anger and forgiveness rather than resentment. Handling stress in a positive way and with a peaceful countenance models Christ before your husband's eyes.

✔ Attend church. Be a part of a small group of Christians with whom you can study God's Word, be accountable, share, and pray one for another.

- ✔ Drink and eat healthy foods. It's been proven that food affects our mood. Eat God's healthy choices instead of processed foods. Practice self-control rather than indulgence.

- ✔ Get enough sleep. Sleep affects our ability to handle stress. It affects our moods. It is important to our health.

- ✔ Exercise. In the first century, it wasn't necessary to tell people to exercise. People walked. They did heavy labor. Why is exercise important? It helps us be more physically and mentally fit. In addition, even a brisk walk elevates the natural feel-good hormones that affect our emotions.

- ✔ Reflect Christ's joy in your relationships. Find someone you enjoy being around, who smiles, and with whom you can laugh. Develop a sense of humor. God must have a sense of humor by the shapes and colors of the animals He created. Jesus used hyperboles and exaggerations. Also, find and read wholesome books, and watch uplifting programs.

5. Which of the above do you most need to do? ________________________________

____

____

Marriage Principle 4

6. We've already read that wives and husbands are to be subject to one another. What principle or tip does Colossians 3:18 and Ephesians 5:22 give for how to be subject to our husbands? ________________________________

____

____

Our fourth principle is to be subject to our husbands "as to the Lord," or "as is fitting in the Lord." Paul didn't give this principle lightly. He knew the challenge of being subject to someone he didn't respect. We see this in Acts 23:1–5. Paul had a hard time being subject to the misguided, arrogant priests and council members before whom he was brought. Although they tried his patience, Paul modeled submission "as to the Lord," even as he wrote to tell believers to submit to one to another.

Although Paul is a good example of submitting to those in authority, Christ is our ultimate model of submitting "as to the Lord." If the hair bristles on the back of our necks at the idea of submitting to our husbands, we do well to remember that without institutions and authorities our world would be in chaos. The Bible doesn't teach that men are better than women. Paul explains in Christ "there is neither male nor female; for you are all one in Christ Jesus" (Galatians 3:28). However, the Bible also explains God has established governing authorities and institutions (Acts 13:1–14), marriage being one such institution. Just as Christ submitted to authority and by His submission, God fulfilled His will through Jesus; so God can fulfill His will through us as we submit to our husbands "as to the Lord."

Is it possible we will ever experience difficult times in marriage or perhaps even suffer through difficult days? Yes. Christ suffered while He was on earth. However, Hebrews 5:8 says Jesus learned obedience by the things He suffered. Jesus didn't waste His suffering. Let's not waste ours. Let's look for how God wants to use us in and through any trial or challenge we may experience. (1 Peter 4:13–14, 16, 19; 5:10)

Marriage Principle 5

7. What is our fifth principle regarding marriage? (Matthew 19:3–8)
   - ❑ God created marriage between Adam and Eve (a man and a woman).
   - ❑ God created marriage between Adam and Steve (same-sex marriage).

Our fifth principle is that God created marriage to be between one man and one woman. Notice Jesus quoted Genesis 1:27; 2:24; and 5:2. Those who discount the authority and reliability of the Old Testament should consider that the Lord Jesus, to whom they have entrusted their souls, honors the Old Testament's authorship and principle that marriage is the union of one man and one woman.

8. What happens to those who pervert God's institution of heterosexual union? (Romans 1:18, 21, 24–28)
   - ❑ God gives them over to a depraved mind.
   - ❑ God blesses them.

Marriage Principle 6

9. What is the sixth principle regarding marriage? (Matthew 19:5–6)
   - ❑ God joins a husband and wife as one flesh.
   - ❑ In marriage, the husband and wife remain two.

The image of God joining a man and woman into one flesh is powerful! Marriage is not to be taken lightly. That's why Christians are commanded to marry believers and not to be bound to darkness. It's one of many reasons we don't "sleep around."

Marriage Principle 7

10. What is a seventh principle regarding marriage? (Matthew 19:6–8)
    - ❑ Man is not to separate what God has joined.
    - ❑ Man is free to separate what God has joined.

Our seventh principle is that God didn't create marriage with a divorce clause. We're not to interfere in other people's marriages nor are they to interfere in ours. Divorce is a result of hardened hearts. If your marriage is in trouble, please go to God and seek His wisdom. Ask Him to show you what's going on with you and your spouse. Be humble, teachable, and obedient.

11. Is a woman free to leave an adulterous husband? (Matthew 19:9)
    ❑ Yes ❑ No

12. Is a woman commanded to leave an adulterous husband?
    ❑ Yes ❑ No

A woman is free, but not commanded to leave her husband if he commits adultery. I've known numerous women and men who've forgiven their spouses of adultery and whose marriages are strong today. Does God expect you to stay in an abusive marriage? No. A woman who is being abused should immediately get help. Once abuse starts, it escalates. Don't be afraid or embarrassed to ask for help. Help is available. God wants to help you. Talk to someone or call National Domestic Violence Hotline at 1-800-799-SAFE (7233) or TTY 1-800-787-3224

Marriage Principle 8

13. What's an eighth principle found in Matthew 19:11–12?
    ❑ Everyone is supposed to get married.
    ❑ Not everyone will get married. Singleness and celibacy is a viable option.

Jesus is an example of one who chose singleness and celibacy. He had no children. He lived an abundant life to the praise of God's glory. Today, for the first time in the history of the United States, married couples are in the minority. The question is: are those who are unmarried remaining celibate; are they remaining pure? Certainly some singles are following Jesus's example and God's commands, yet many are not.

What's in Your Basket?

Basket Case

- I haven't known God's principles for marriage.
- I ignore God's principles for marriage.

Extraordinary Life

- I'm following God's principles for marriage as best as I can.
- Though not always easy, I try to submit to my husband, as to the Lord.

Basket Case

- My husband is ignoring God's principles for marriage.
- My child is ignoring God's principles for marriage.

Extraordinary Life

- I pray for my husband regularly, for our love to grow and that our marriage be to God's glory.
- I pray for my child to follow God's principles for marriage.

♦ *Perhaps I'm a basket case because I hadn't studied God's principles for marriage and I'm suffering the consequences of bad choices.*
♦ *Perhaps I'm a basket case because I've known God's principles for marriage, but I've ignored them and done what I wanted to do.*
♦ *Perhaps I'm a basket case because my children are ignoring God's principles for marriage and I worry about them.*
♦ *Perhaps I'm a basket case because I'm not married and I want to be.*
♦ *Perhaps I'm a basket case because I'm married and I wish I were not.*

Thinking It Over

♥ 1. Which principle for marriage do you think: ______

a) Is the most awesome? ______

b) Is the hardest to follow? ______

c) Is the most ignored by your nation? ______

♥ 2. Which principle do you want to make a matter of prayer for yourself or someone else? ______

______

♥ 3. What verse would be good for you to remember? Why? ______

______

Day 3: *More Biblical Principles for Marriage*

Father, thank You for Your Word and the insights and reminders You give me through it. Help me be a woman who honors You in singleness or marriage. In Jesus's name. Amen.

♦ ♦ ♦

Mary's parents talked for a long time after listening to Paul's words about marriage. His words were liberating for her mother! The following days she noticed a spring in her step. When Mary asked her about it, she replied, "Just cooking as unto the Lord! Just cleaning as unto the Lord!" The twinkle in her mother's eyes that had faded through the years returned.

◆ ◆ ◆

Paul ached for his friends and co-workers who were struggling in their marriages. Often, a husband would feel God impressing him to go on a missions trip, but his wife didn't want him to go. At other times, a woman would want to offer her home as a meeting place for believers, but her husband refused. Some husbands became jealous of their wives' relationship with Jesus Christ. Other men were overly demanding of their wives and unforgiving of their faults. He prayed his words would penetrate their hearts.

◆ ◆ ◆

Marriage is wonderful but it is also tough work! Men and women are wired differently. That makes for excitement *and* misunderstandings. The hope is that Christian marriages can be examples to others. Regardless of the current condition of our marriages, with Christ's help, they can improve. As we continue looking at God's principles for marriage, let's make these principles a matter of prayer.

Marriage Principle 9

Yesterday we looked at the principle of mutual submission in marriage and how women are to submit to their husbands as to the Lord. It is a continuation of the theme that Christ is our life and that everything we do, we do in honor and obedience as unto Him (Colossians 3:17).

1. What was on God's mind when He created Eve for Adam? (Genesis 2:18)
   - ❑ Eve would be a hindrance to Adam.
   - ❑ Eve would be a helper to Adam.

In Genesis 2:18 we see a biblical principle that might make some women go ballistic.

"Helper? How dare we be called helpers! How about my husband help me?" some might retort, especially if one is in a difficult marriage. Please remember the principles we're studying are God's principles and that sin has marred God's institutions. However, we can still embrace God's design for marriage and model Christian marriages to the next generation.

2. If you don't like the sound of *helper*, please note with whom you share that title. Please record who is called a helper. (John 14:16; 15:26) ____________________

Helper is one of the ways God has chosen to refer to Himself. I'd say we're honored to share His title. God knew Adam needed a helper, and He created woman. God knew we needed a helper, and He gave us the Holy Spirit, the Helper. Rather than resist our divinely appointed calling, let's humbly fall on our faces and fulfill our role with gratitude.

When I studied these verses years ago, they revolutionized my thinking. They helped me as I went about my work and when Keith asked me to do something. In addition, understanding my role as Keith's helper has become a lighthearted issue in our marriage. If we don't see eye-to-eye on something, I remind Keith that God knew he needed a helper and I'm it!

Marriage Principle 10

3. Wives are to relate to their husbands as the church does to Christ (Ephesians 5:24). What word defines that relationship? (Ephesians 5:33) ____________________

Our tenth principle is: Wives are to respect their husbands.

Keith and I have a funny story about the word *respect*. Although we didn't laugh at the time, we do now. The first time Keith told me he loved me it came as a surprise to me. Although we'd been dating for some time, I had no idea he felt that way. I liked Keith, but was caught off guard and responded with what I truly felt for him, "I respect you." That wasn't exactly the response for which he'd hoped. He immediately began backpedaling and tried to explain how he just "liked me a lot." Although I felt terrible, I couldn't honestly tell him I loved him. I did respect him, though, and my respect grew into love.

During our more than 30 years of marriage, there have been times when, in the heat of an argument, neither of us have "felt love" for each other. But a day has never gone by that I've not respected Keith. Moms, we can teach our daughters to marry a man they respect. Then, when he says, "I think God wants us to move" or when life is confusing, she can pray for him and respect how God leads him. I've been shocked and dismayed at how many parents teach their daughters to look for a spouse who has money or a great job, but neglect the weightier issue of respect. Appearances will fade. Money can be lost. Character is golden. Teach your daughters to go for the gold. Our daughter, Lauren, married a few years ago. Keith and I thank God for Chris, a man we all respect.

Marriage Principle 11

Have you ever misunderstood your husband, child, or co-worker? Sometimes we hear things differently than they were intended. The biblical principles for marriage are a case in point. Some women, when they read the word "submit," visualize an overbearing husband making unrealistic demands. Can you relate to the following cartoon?

On the other hand, Keith can't find anything in the refrigerator. The mustard could jump out and squirt itself on his shirt and he would stand there with the door open and ask me where it is. Bless his heart. I'm not impatient anymore. It helps to have more than 30 years under my belt. We've both come to terms with each other's idiosyncrasies. This brings us to the next wonderful principle!

4. Read Colossians 3:19. What's the 11th principle regarding husbands and wives?

____

____

Our eleventh principle is: Husbands are to love their wives. Paul spends a great deal of time explaining the husband's role. As a matter of fact, he repeats three times: husbands are to love their wives. Might that be because he knew men wouldn't be listening the first two times?

5. Read Ephesians 5:23–25, 28–29, 33. What pressure husbands do have! How did Paul qualify the love husbands are to have for their wives?

   Ephesians 5:25 ______________________________

   Ephesians 5:28 ______________________________

   Ephesians 5:33 ______________________________

According to *The Discovery Bible,* the word used for love in these verses is *agapao,* which means "to love dearly."

Agape love:

- ❑ Refers to an "unselfish, outgoing affection or tenderness for another without necessarily expecting anything in return."

- ❑ Seeks a person's highest good on the basis of a decision of will and an inclination of heart.
- ❑ Is "a self-giving personal commitment irrespective of grateful response."

Agape love is different from *phileo* love, which, according to *The Discovery Bible,* "denotes a loving friendship based on common interests, often accompanied by warm feelings and affection."

When a husband loves his wife with self-sacrificing love, a wife isn't going to balk when he makes a request. The husband's not going to be overly demanding. He's going to be mindful of her commitments, needs, and interests. He's going to be a prayer warrior who battles for her sanctity and displays love toward her. No, he's not going to be perfect; but neither are we.

Moms raising young boys can start grooming them for their high calling as godly men and potential husbands. Parents raising teen boys can model a godly marriage. Those who have adult sons can share these biblical teachings with them and pray these Scriptures for their sons and their spouses. Parents can also share Christian devotional books for couples, by placing those in their guest room.

What do you do if your husband isn't knowledgeable about the Scriptures that pertain to his role or his heart isn't quickened to the need to obey them? Begin praying them for him. Keep a devotional book for couples on your breakfast table. He might glance at it after you go to bed. If he is open to your concerns, share with him what you're learning. Tell him you want to be the godly wife God has called you to be. Pray that the Lord stirs his heart to love you sacrificially as Christ loved the church.

6. What's your prayer? ____

____

____

Marriage Principle 12

7. What's an additional principle for husbands? (Colossians 3:19) Check one.
   - ❑ Be embittered against your wife.
   - ❑ Do not be embittered against your wife.

Embittered here means "exasperated, rendered angry, indignant, irritated." Hebrews 12:15 warns against a root of bitterness springing up that can cause trouble. Ephesians 4:31–32 says put bitterness, wrath, anger, clamor, slander, and malice away from you; be kind, tenderhearted, "forgiving each other, just as God in Christ also has forgiven you."

8. Why do you think the Bible tells husbands not to be bitter toward their wives?

____

____

9. Without giving names, do you know anyone who is embittered against his wife?
   ❑ Yes ❑ No

10. Do you know any woman who is embittered, angry, indignant, and irritated with her husband?
   ❑ Yes ❑ No

11. How do you think Jesus would counsel the husbands and wives? ________________

____

____

What's in Your Basket?

Basket Case

- Hate the concept of being my husband's helper
- Resent my husband
- Given up on my husband

Extraordinary Life

- Love the concept of being my husband's helper
- Respect my husband
- Pray for my husband

♦ *Perhaps I'm a basket case because I've gotten away from what should be a wife's biblical perspective.*

♦ *Perhaps I'm a basket case because I assume my husband is always critical of me. As a matter of fact, I think he's bitter toward me.*

♦ *Perhaps I'm a basket case because my husband thinks I'm critical and controlling.*

♦ *Perhaps I'm a basket case because I often hear and perceive comments my husband makes from a negative, defensive perspective. I assume my husband is being critical when he is not.*

Thinking It Over

♥ 1. Have you heard people talk negatively about Paul because they've misunderstood his teaching about a wife being submissive to her husband? How would you explain these verses to people? ________________

____

♥ 2. How is God speaking to you through today's Scriptures? What principles or truths do you want to remember? ________________

____

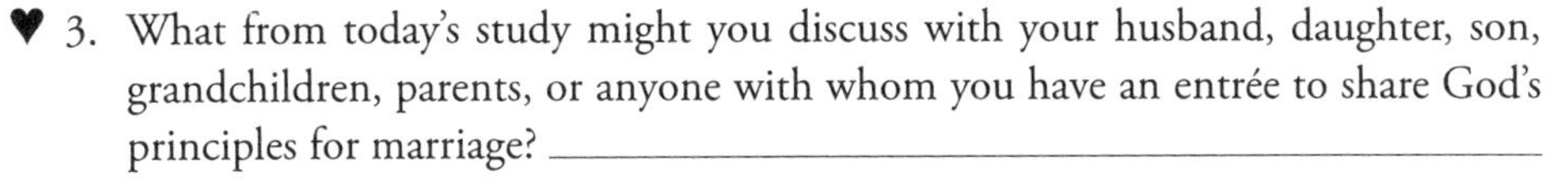

♥ 3. What from today's study might you discuss with your husband, daughter, son, grandchildren, parents, or anyone with whom you have an entrée to share God's principles for marriage? ______________________________

____

Day 4: *The Excellent Wife, Who Can Find Her?*

Father, thank You for shining Your Light on my life and heart. Continue to teach me Your ways. Inspire and fill me so that I serve You in an extraordinary way. In Jesus's name. Amen.

◆ ◆ ◆

Rachel was bursting with enthusiasm over her enlightenment courses! Mary was finding it more and more difficult to enjoy Rachel's company. However, she felt it important to maintain their friendship. "Perhaps, one day, when Rachel tires of seeking to find her own deity, she'll turn to Christ," Mary confided in her mother.

Rachel begged Mary to join her for the weekend at Hierapolis. "The baths are perfect places to meet people…men or women," she gushed. Mary was dismayed at what Rachel's invitation implied. She didn't want to find a man at a bath and she certainly had no intention of finding a woman. She politely declined and, in turn, instead invited Rachel to church to hear a second reading of Paul's letter. Rachel declined.

◆ ◆ ◆

In Paul's younger years, he had assumed he would become a married man with a house full of children. Now, unmarried, he sat in prison. Though he sometimes yearned for a wife's companionship, he knew the grass was not "always greener on the other side." Marriage meant not only companionship, but also responsibility. With his full attention directed to serving Christ, Paul knew he was where he needed to be. "Thank You, Lord, that I'm single and can serve You with singleness of devotion."

◆ ◆ ◆

The Proverbs 31 Woman

Yesterday, we examined the biblical role of a husband. Today, we're studying the biblical role of a wife. Let's begin by looking at the Proverbs 31 woman, who embodies the essence of a godly woman and wife. Please take a moment to read verses 10–31.

1. This woman is amazing! Is she real?
   - ❑ Yes. She's in the Bible.
   - ❑ No. He said, "Who can find her?"
   - ❑ I don't know.

Whether she was real or is an ideal, let's try to put the Proverbs 31 woman in perspective, because obviously, she's in the Bible as a model for us.

2. How does the author describe an excellent woman's worth, compared to jewels? (Proverbs31:10)____

This man is describing a woman whom he values more than money.

3. What makes her so special? Is it because she's a hard worker? (Proverbs 31:11)

I can almost see the husband in Proverbs 31, looking at his wife. He isn't looking at her makeup or hair. He isn't noticing those few extra pounds she has put on. He's looking at her heart. He trusts her.

4. What does Peter remind us of in 1 Peter 3:3? Please personalize your answer.

   My adornment must not be merely ____

5. What are some ways you adorn yourself externally? ______________________________

Peter doesn't say we're not to adorn or take care of ourselves physically. As a matter of fact, it's important for people, including Christian women, to take care of themselves. Our bodies are the temple of the Holy Spirit and our appearance should honor Him (1 Corinthians 6:19–20).

6. What does Peter point to as more important than a woman's external adornment? (1 Peter 3:4) ____

Underline those words, for they are rich indeed! God looks at our hearts. So do others. They can't help to do so. We wear our heart in our eyes. We wear our hearts in our facial expressions. Are we angry? It shows. Is bitterness lurking in the crevices of our hearts? It shows.

The Hidden Person of the Heart

7. How does 1 Peter 3:4 describe "the hidden person of the heart" with whom we should adorn ourselves? ____

I want to be like this; to have what Peter describes as "the imperishable quality of a gentle and quiet spirit." What about you?

I remember, when I was a little girl, telling Mama how beautiful she was. At the time, she was up to her elbows in dishwater. I have no idea what she was wearing. I was looking at her countenance. Her response: "You just think I'm pretty because I'm you're mommy." In other words, it was her heart I loved, not her external adornment.

If a wife—or a potential wife—wants a husband to love her, perhaps she should be prepared to do more than care for children, pay the bills, or accomplish specific jobs each day. Perhaps we should place higher value on meeting with God every day. He's the only one who can create in us a beauty that's imperishable. Meeting with a trainer, if we can afford one, and carving out the time to get our bodies in shape has merit. Yet, meeting with God is free and has greater merit. We can't afford not to meet with Him if we want the imperishable quality Peter describes and the Proverbs 31 woman models.

Our heart; a godly husband falls in love with his wife's *heart*.

8. How does God view one who has a gentle and quiet spirit?
   ❑ As productive ❑ As precious in His sight

Having a gentle and quiet spirit is not synonymous with weakness or being a doormat. There's more strength in a woman who's able to control her tongue than a woman who can't.

What's in Your Basket?

Basket Case

- Adorned externally
- Harsh, uncontrolled spirit
- Put everything ahead of God, as well as my husband

Extraordinary Life

- Adornment is external and in the hidden person of my heart.
- Gentle, quiet spirit
- Give time to God and to my husband

♦ *Perhaps I'm a basket case because I don't tend to the hidden person of the heart.*
♦ *Perhaps I'm a basket case because my internal adornment isn't beautiful and my husband is not attracted to my external adornment either.*

Thank You, Lord, that, through You, I can work on both my internal and external adornment. Thank You, Lord, that You're the beauty in me. Train my thoughts, tongue, and heart so they're precious in Your sight. In Jesus's name. Amen.

Thinking It Over

♥ 1. Whether you're married or single, how is God speaking to you about the person He wants you to be? ______

______

♥ 2. Rather than regret the past, repent of anything you regret. Repent means to agree with God and change directions. Start fresh today. Follow God's teachings. In what way is God calling you to follow Him? ______

______

♥ 3. What golden nugget and verse do you want to remember? Why? Thank God for how He is growing you in Him! ______

______

Day 5: *Parents and Children*

Father, we're hungry to know Your ways. Please teach us Your vision for parent/child relationships and help us walk in them. In Jesus's name. Amen.

♦ ♦ ♦

Mary's mother wanted to hug Paul's neck for the godly counsel he was giving! "Listen, children!" she wanted to say. "Listen, dear!"

♦ ♦ ♦

Paul's sister was on his mind more and more often. He wondered how she was. As he thought about his family, he reflected on his childhood years and the strong hand with which his father led their family. He was a good man, knowledgeable of God's Word, and passionate to uphold the faith. Although he had at times been stern with Paul, his parents had helped shape and prepare him for the course his life would take.

♦ ♦ ♦

Read Colossians 3:20–21.

Now look at these statistics from the US Census Bureau (March 2008)

33 percent	This is the percentage of births in 2002 to unmarried women. The rate varies from 89 percent for unmarried teenagers aged 15 to 19, to 12 percent for unmarried women aged 30 to 44.

12.2 million	This is the number of single parents: 10 million single mothers and 2.2 million single fathers.
43 percent	Percentage of opposite-sex, unmarried partner households that include children.
683,000	Number of unmarried grandparents who are responsible for caring for their grandchildren. These grandparents comprise nearly 1 in 3 unmarried grandparents.

To those who are single parents, God has a special word of encouragement.

1. Read Psalm 146, focusing on verse 9. Who does the Lord support?

____

2. Read Psalm 68:5. How is God described? ______________________________

____

3. Read Psalm 68:6. For whom does God make a home?
   ❑ The proud ❑ The lonely

We are aware of the changes in family structure and the US Census Bureau statistics confirm that the so-called *Ozzie and Harriet* nuclear family is from an era gone by. As Christians, we must embrace the present child rearing challenges with the courage and resources God gives us. We must also do what we can to turn the tide to God's ideal, to do what we can to have an impact on our generation for Christ.

A wise woman once told me we can't go back, but we can start where we are with God and do things His way. That's good news for all of us. I know few parents who don't regret some aspect of how they raised their children. We do well to remember that there is not a perfect parent and even the best of parents won't raise a perfect child. However, we can start where we are, regardless of our children's ages, and present a positive influence on them for Christ.

4. What does Colossians 3:20 command children to do? ______________________

5. Who is pleased when children obey? (Colossians 3:20)
   ❑ Santa Claus ❑ The Lord

Children may be taught that Santa Claus is watching them and knows whether they're naughty or nice. They may hear that if they're good, Santa Claus will reward them with presents. If they're bad, he won't. I've often wondered why adults eagerly teach children a fable yet fail to teach children that God sees whether they're being naughty or nice and is pleased when they're obedient.

6. Do you teach your children that God sees their behavior and is pleased when they obey?
   ❑ Yes ❑ No ❑ A little

Thank You, Father, that it's never too late to teach our children. We can lovingly teach our children that God sees them and is pleased when they obey. We can reinforce good behavior with smiles, hugs, and words of affirmation. For example, "God saw how quickly you obeyed Mommy and is so pleased with you!"

If your children are grown and you regret some way in which you raised them, apologize. "I'm sorry," goes a long way. In addition, it opens the door to discuss additional spiritual subjects pertinent to them as adults. We can share with children of any age what we're learning and how it is having a positive impact on our lives.

If you don't have children, you still influence those around you in ways you may not even realize. Whether with children in your extended family, the children's program at your church, a mentoring program at a school, or one of the many agencies who care for children, there are numerous opportunities to influence children for Christ!

7. Parents have a responsibility to do more for their children than teach them to brush their teeth, get an education, and be responsible. What powerful commands did God give parents in Deuteronomy 6:5–7?

   a) Deuteronomy 6:5 ____________________________________

   b) Deuteronomy 6:6 ____________________________________

   c) Deuteronomy 6:7 ____________________________________

8. How are parents to teach their children? (Deuteronomy 6:7) ________________

____

Diligently carries the idea of "sharpening, whetting, teaching incisively."

9. When are parents to diligently teach their children about God? Check all that apply. Underline when you diligently teach your children. (Deuteronomy 6:7)
   ❑ When you sit in your house ❑ When you walk by the way
   ❑ When you lie down ❑ When you rise up

The purpose of our study isn't to make any of us feel guilty if we have failed to follow God's teaching in Deuteronomy. Rather, the purpose of our study is to know what God teaches us so that we can obey Him, as well as influence others to follow Him. God's Word sharpens us. It teaches us what we need to know in order to be good parents, citizens, church members, spouses, employees, and friends.

You may agree that parenting is one of the hardest jobs a person does, yet most of us receive little training for how to be a good parent. However, the Bible gives us instructions. We can soak in God's Word, trusting its counsel, and in turn, teach our children.

Deuteronomy 6:7 doesn't have to be an overwhelming undertaking. God isn't telling us to enroll our children in an expensive institution for biblical learning. Rather, it teaches us to talk with our children about God throughout the natural course of the day.

Some of my fondest memories of teaching Taylor and Lauren about God are when they were infants and I nursed them. While nursing and rocking them, I sang hymns to them. They grew up saying bedtime, morning, and mealtime prayers. On walks, we talked about all the wonderful things God created—the rocks, leaves, flowers. I taught Taylor to say, "Thank You, Lord, for the birds." Keith taught Taylor how to *shoot* the birds. Was it any wonder when Taylor was five and asked to set up Kidz Time, an A to Z devotional activity I wrote, he chose 1 Timothy 4:4 (paraphrased), "Everything God made is good and we may eat it gladly if we are thankful." Needless to say, Keith smiled at our young son's application of God's Word.

When you speak of God naturally during the course of the day, your children absorb more than you realize. Once, after being out of town with Keith, Keith's mother babysat for us. She later told me how she had held our three-year-old Lauren in her arms and had taken her to look out the window. When she did, Lauren said, "Thank You, Lord, for this beautiful day." Grace thought it was so cute. I was moved beyond words. What Lauren had heard me say every morning as I showed her the new day had taken root in her little heart.

10. We take time and energy to teach our children to brush teeth, tie shoelaces, and button shirts. Why would we think it less important to teach them the daily disciplines of reading their Bibles and praying? ______________________

11. Someone might ask, "If I send my kids to church every Sunday, is that sufficient spiritual training?" How would you answer on the basis of Deuteronomy 6:7?

____

____

- *Perhaps my kids are basket cases because I haven't raised them to know and think of God during the day. Instead, they associate God with a church building and a day of the week.*
- *Perhaps my kids are basket cases because I tried to cram God's Word down their throats instead of letting His life and words flow naturally during the course of our day with both structured Bible and prayertime as well as impromptu discussions about God.*

12. What warning does Colossians 3:21 give fathers, which also applies to mothers?

____

____

13. What is the logic of not exasperating or provoking your children? What can happen to children if parents exasperate them? ______

Colossians 3:21 ______

Ephesians 6:4 ______

14. How are children to be brought up? (Ephesians 6:4) ______

Friends, we're commanded to bring up our children in the discipline and instruction of the Lord. It's to be part of our general habit or home lifestyle. It's to be a long-term commitment.

15. What's the reward of raising children in the instruction and discipline of the Lord and of them obeying and honoring you? (Ephesians 6:3) ______

What if you're a single parent, or married to an unbeliever who isn't committed to diligently teach your children? Just as Timothy's mother and grandmother taught him, you can still teach them (2 Timothy 1:5). You can pray for God to bring spiritual mentors into their lives, even as Paul was a mentor to Timothy.

If we train our children in the instruction and discipline of the Lord, does it mean they'll never stray? No. All people sin and fall short of the glory of God, so we know there are no perfect children. Many well-intentioned, godly parents have felt confused because they raised their children to know God, yet their children wandered away from God. How do we understand Proverbs 22:6 when children stray from the godly training parents have given them? *The Bible Knowledge Commentary* explains in the following way:

> A proverb is a literary device whereby a general truth is brought to bear on a specific situation.... Though the proverbs are generally and usually true, occasional exceptions may be noted. This may be because of the self-will or deliberate disobedience of an individual who chooses to go his own way.... It *is* generally true, however, that most children who are brought up in Christian homes, under the influence of godly parents who teach and live God's standards (Eph. 6:4), follow that training.

Certainly, children will be grateful to parents who love them enough to instill God's values in their hearts. Such parents not only give physical life to their children, but also inspire spiritual life. There's no more important work a parent can do than introduce their children to the Lord Jesus Christ!

What's in Your Basket?

Basket Case

- Overwhelmed with commitments; no time to teach my children about God
- Forget my children have a heavenly Father who is watching over them

Extraordinary Life

- Prayerfully balance commitments; make time to teach my children about God
- Thankful my children have a heavenly Father who's watching over them

♦ *Perhaps I'm a basket case because I'm overwhelmed with all there is to do to raise a child.*

♦ *Perhaps I'm a basket case because I don't have any help. I'm a single parent or might as well be. My husband doesn't help.*

♦ *Perhaps I'm a basket case because I make raising my children to know the Lord too hard a task. I need to step back, take a deep breath, meet with God in the mornings, and then teach them what He's teaching me as we're eating meals, driving places, involved in activities, and preparing to rest at home.*

♦ *Perhaps I'm a basket case because I forget my children have a heavenly Father. He is watching over them.*

Thinking It Over

♥ 1. How is God's Word an encouragement to single parents?

____

____

____

♥ 2. What points do you want to remember from today's study?

____

____

____

♥ 3. If you don't have children or your children are grown and you have grandchildren, how could you apply today's verses?

____

____

____

Weekly Wrap-Up

Where Am I? With which basket-case point from this week's study do I most relate?

____

____

____

Where Do I Want to Be? To which aspects of extraordinary living is God calling me?

____

____

____

How Will I Get There? What golden nugget and/or verse from this week's study do I want to remember to help me better handle my basket-case moments and live an extraordinary life?

____

____

____

Thinking of Others: What from this week's study do I want to share with someone to encourage or warn them?

____

____

____

Biblical Questions and Answers About Sex, Singles, Second Marriages, and Sexual Immorality

1. What does God teach about sex within marriage? (1 Corinthians 7:1–5)

✔ Verse 2 Sex is to be practiced between one man and one woman in the context of marriage: husband and wife.

✔ Verses 3–4 Husbands and wives are to fulfill their sexual duty to one another.

✔ Verse 5 Husbands and wives are not to deprive one another of sex.

✔ Verse 5 Husbands and wives may abstain from sex for a period of time they both agree upon in order to devote themselves to prayer.

✔ Verse 5 Those who deprive one another of sex should be aware that Satan may tempt one or both of you.

2. What does God teach about singleness? (1 Corinthians 7:7–9, 32–35)

✔ Verse 7 Each person has his or her own calling from God—to singleness or marriage.

✔ Verse 8 Singleness is good because the single person's interests aren't divided between God and the person to whom they're married. The single person can give undistracted devotion to God.

3. What does the Bible teach about second marriages for widows? (1 Corinthians 7:39–40)

✔ Verse 39 A widow is free to marry whom she wishes, as long as the person is a Christian.

✔ Verse 40 Paul's personal opinion is she'll be happier if she doesn't remarry. However, he clearly states that is just his opinion.

What does the Bible teach about sexual immorality: adultery, homosexuality, and fornication?

(1 Corinthians 6:9–10; 1 Timothy 1:10; Revelation 21:7–8; 22:14–19)

✔ Adultery, fornication, and the sexual practice of homosexuality are sins. Christians do not want to practice sin. They want to practice righteousness. Christ died that we might be washed of sin. Therefore, it's inconsistent for a Christian to presume that sins for which Christ died are acceptable to practice. We deceive ourselves with such unbiblical conclusions.

♦ WEEK 8 ♦

BASKET CASE OR EXTRAORDINARY?

This week, as we are concluding this study, our hearts and minds are blessed with the "icing on the cake"—*how* we can live extraordinary lives for God. Be blessed as you study!

♦ ♦ ♦

As Paul drew near the end of his letter, he thought back on what he had written. He prayed that the believers were stronger in their faith.

♦ ♦ ♦

Mary woke with Rachel on her mind. She'd come to realize Rachel wasn't going to attend church with her—at least not any time soon. With that realization, she decided to take God's Word to Rachel. Mary asked God to open doors for her to share His truths with her, "Lord, please give me words to respond to Rachel when she insists her crystals hold all the power she needs."

Later, Mary excitedly told her mother. "I'm going to tell Rachel I'm wearing something, too, that brings power to my life: the Lord Jesus Christ!" With renewed zeal, Mary hurried out the door.

♦ ♦ ♦

DAY 1: *Biblical Principles for Work, Part 1*

Father, thank You for the privilege of coming to You. Thank You for Your arms, which are always open to receive me. Help me view work as something You've entrusted to me. Help me serve You with a sincere heart. In Jesus's name. Amen.

♦ ♦ ♦

"Onesimus, you must return to Philemon, your rightful master. I've written him, informing him you've accepted Christ as your Savior and asking him to be merciful to you. In addition, I've offered to pay any debt you owe. When you arrive, work heartily for him as though you are serving the Lord." With parting words, Onesimus returned to Philemon.

Mary was sorry to see Onesimus leave, but knew it was right for him to go.

♦ ♦ ♦

READ COLOSSIANS 3:22 TO 4:1.

When Paul wrote Colossians, slavery was an established institution in the Roman Empire. As a matter of fact, according to pastor and author Warren Wiersbe, there were 60 million slaves. Many were well-educated people with great responsibility, who served in the homes of the wealthy and helped to educate and discipline the children.

Christianity introduced a new perspective on slaves and masters. Masters were no longer to treat slaves as objects, but rather as fellow heirs of salvation. Slaves were not to halfheartedly serve their masters, but were to work as if they were serving the Lord.

How do we address these verses today? May I suggest that we substitute *employee* in the place of *slave* and *employer* in the place of *master*? For those who work outside the home, this will be easy. For those who are not employed outside the home, you one day may be, so it serves you well to hide these verses in your heart. If you have children, grandchildren, or mentor someone, you can teach them these principles.

Work Principle 1

1. Everyone on earth has a "master," someone "over" him or her. (Colossians 3:22; 4:1)
   ❑ True ❑ False

Work Principle 2

2. There are earthly masters and a heavenly Master. (Colossians 3:22; 4:1)
   ❑ True ❑ False

Work Principle 3

3. The key word for how an employee is to relate to their employer: Colossians 3:22.
   ❑ Rebel ❑ Obey

In our study of verses 20–21 previously, Paul emphasized the importance of children being obedient to their parents. Obedience to authority is foundational to all relationships.

4. Do you find it easier to "let something go" with children, an employee, or committee member rather than to hold the person accountable?
   ❑ Yes. I find it hard to hold someone accountable.
   ❑ No. I find it easy to hold people accountable.

5. In order to hold someone accountable, it's imperative to have clearly defined expectations. Do you clearly define your expectations and set "due" dates?
   ❑ Yes ❑ No

6. Which is more difficult for you? Defining expectations or holding someone accountable to expectations you've set? ______________________________

Work Principle 4

7. Our goal in regard to work is to
   ❑ Perform external service, as people pleasers
   ❑ Serve with sincerity of heart, fearing the Lord

This is an important principle. I'm sure you've heard the story of the child who refused to sit down during class, eventually sat down, but defiantly announced he was standing up on the inside.

I wonder how many of us have adopted that mind-set? We may complete our responsibilities, but resent the person in authority over us. Colossians 3:22 challenges us to serve others with a sincere heart, fearing the Lord.

8. Check the following descriptions of "man pleasers" who don't serve with sincerity of heart.
   ❑ They resent the person over them.
   ❑ They resent their job.
   ❑ They give external service with an insincere heart.

Paul isn't telling us to ignore our feelings. He's calling us to see God's highest purposes in our work and lives. For instance, when we look to Jesus, our model, we don't find Him smiling at the Pharisees who accused Him of casting out demons by the devil and responding, "Whatever you say." Rather, Jesus rebutted their accusations with clarifying truth. Taking Jesus as our model, we learn that if there's something on our mind in regard to someone with whom we work, rather than be an insincere people pleaser, we should find the right moment to voice our concern, but with sincerity and respect.

9. How might honesty and sincerity of heart drastically improve work relationships?

____

____

____

A friend whom I admire once became upset with her husband. I asked her, "Do you think he knows what he did to upset you?" Her response? "Oh, he knows what he did!" No doubt she was right. However, it caused me to wonder if I ever make assumptions that others know what I mean or how I feel, though they don't. It causes me to make an effort to be the best communicator possible.

10. What happens if employers, parents, spouses, or committee chairpersons don't clearly state expectations? ______________________________

11. What happens when employees, children, spouses, or committee members don't communicate their feelings, but rather hide resentment and work as people pleasers? Check all that apply.
    ❑ Dissatisfaction grows. ❑ Discontentment or resentment festers.

If you're an employer, parent, or committee chairperson, you may have discovered late in a relationship that someone was unhappy with you. Perhaps they didn't like a ministry direction you took. Maybe they thought your meetings should have been longer, shorter, more often, less often—yet they never told you. If you're an employer, parent, or chairperson, you may know the feeling of betrayal when you sincerely ask for opinions and comments, don't receive them, and then find that someone harbored resentment toward you in an area that could have been changed.

Closer to home, sometimes children may appear to be doing all the right things, while hiding a life of promiscuity or drug use. Or, a wife can tell her husband that everything is fine, though she is making plans secretly to meet with another man. Husbands can fake being happily married, then announce one day they're leaving the marriage. These are not God's ways.

12. Who is someone with whom you live or work but harbor ill will or discontentment toward? ______________________________ (Give one initial only)

13. Why do you think God wants sincerity of heart to be part of your relationship?

____

____

14. Are you doing yourself or the other person a favor by hiding your thoughts and feelings?
    ❑ Yes ❑ No

15. What fear prevents you from speaking with the person about what's on your mind?

____

____

Matthew 18:15–20 has excellent principles regarding relationships. What do you do if a difference of opinion—not sin—is causing relationship problems? What if the person isn't a Christian? What if you fear losing your job?

Prayerfully consider the following Scriptures in light of your situation.

- Matthew 5:43–44, 47, gives the law of love. It instructs us to pray for our enemies and greet not only our "brothers" but also others.
- Matthew 7:3–5 teaches us to take the log out of our eye before we try to remove the speck out of our brother's eye. In other words, we are to prayerfully consider if we have any part in the unhealthy relationship. If so, what?
- Ephesians 4:15 gives sound advice: speak the truth in love. We must check our hearts. Are we jealous or angry? We must check our motives. Are they pure? We must check our ultimate aim. Is it to serve God's purposes?
- We must recognize nonbelievers don't have the same values as Christians. Therefore, we shouldn't be shocked when they don't adhere to our moral values. With unbelieving employers, parents, or leaders, we have the opportunity to show the Light of Christ. (Matthew 5:16)

Work Principle 5

16. How are Christians to work? (Colossians 3:23) ______________________________

____

This is a verse that the Holy Spirit brings to my mind when I'm faced with tasks I don't want to do. I meditate on it when I'm weary but have work yet to be completed. It is relatively easy to memorize and definitely worth it as it makes so much sense! If our lives are Christ's, then both menial and important tasks should be done with integrity and without complaining, for we're serving the Lord. If we're exhausted at the end of a long day and tired of taking care of little ones, we can remember that God sees us. What we're doing is important to Him, even if no one else notices. When we work hard at our jobs and someone else gets recognized instead of us, we can know that the Lord sees the good work we did. It's God whom we serve.

Is your employer, husband, or parent overly demanding? Carry these verses in your heart. Pray for the opportunity to have an honest discussion with them.

Work Principle 6

17. What does Colossians 3:23 say to do heartily? ______________________________

That is our sixth principle: work is work! It isn't called fun. Some of us may squirm at the word *work*. We're like Peter Pan. We don't want to grow up. We want to have fun, which may translate into excessive shopping, television, vacationing, reading, talking on the telephone, lazing around, sports, emailing, or Internet surfing. Although none of those are wrong, they're not to control our lives. We're made in God's image with minds and abilities. Rather than balk at work, we can do our work with sincerity of heart as to the Lord.

What's in Your Basket?

Basket Case

- I resent having to work.
- I'm a people pleaser.
- I'm too busy to teach my children responsibility and obedience.

Extraordinary Life

- I understand work is part of God's plan.
- I try to serve others with a sincere heart.
- I teach my children responsibility and obedience.

♦ *Perhaps I'm a basket case because I don't like to work. I don't embrace it as part of my God-given calling.*

♦ *Perhaps I'm a basket case because I don't communicate my feelings. I'm a man pleaser. I want people to know automatically how I feel and what I'm thinking.*

♦ *Perhaps I'm a basket case because I know I should teach my children to follow through with their responsibilities, but I don't.*

Thinking It Over

♥ 1. What has God prompted you to consider regarding work? ____________________

____

♥ 2. Why is it important for Christians to work with sincere hearts? ____________________

____

♥ 3. What golden nugget do you want to remember from today's study? ____________________

____

Day 2: *Biblical Principles for Work, Part 2*

Father, thank You for the fullness and richness of Your Word. Show me today how to be a woman who honors You in all things. In Jesus's name. Amen.

♦ ♦ ♦

Mary gained new appreciation for work after hearing Paul's words. Beforehand, she'd felt imposed on by what others required of her. She had not considered God in relation to work. She had separated work from worship. Now she realized that God saw her at work just as He saw her at worship. Knowing that, she began to work heartily, as if serving Christ.

♦ ♦ ♦

Paul reasoned with his visitor. "Sure, we'll always have others who make unreasonable demands. Remember, however, our ultimate Master is the Lord! It's Him we serve! He will reward us."

◆ ◆ ◆

REREAD COLOSSIANS 3:22 TO 4:1 TO REFRESH YOUR MEMORY OF OUR SCRIPTURES.

According to a February 28, 2005, press release by The Conference Board,

> U.S. Job Satisfaction Keeps Falling.... Americans are growing increasingly unhappy with their jobs.... Half of all Americans today say they are satisfied with their jobs, down from nearly 60 percent in 1995.... Among the 50 percent who say they are content, only 14 percent say they are "very satisfied." ... Forty percent of workers feel disconnected from their employers.... Twenty-five percent of employees are just "showing up to collect a paycheck."

Today, consider your attitude toward work and your employer or employees. In addition to our homes, where better can we be witnesses for Christ?

Work Principle 7

1. What's God's instruction regarding the person who doesn't work? Fill in the blank. (2 Thessalonians 3:10)

   "If anyone is not willing to work, then he is ____________________ to eat either."

   God's principle is simple: Don't work; don't eat.

Work Principle 8

2. What does Genesis 2:2 say that God completed? ____________________

If God hadn't finished His work, perhaps we wouldn't have the flowers or the fish of the sea. However, He did. All we enjoy on earth is the completed work of God's hands (Psalm 19:1). God worked; this is an important principle for us to follow.

It's easy to start something and not finish it. We may begin a project and then leave it unfinished. We do well to train our children to complete their work as well. If we're having trouble completing a task assigned to us, we should pray and ask for help.

3. Who models finishing an incredibly difficult work assignment? (John 19:30)

____

Work Principle 9

4. What did God model and command, which affects our stress, health, and productivity? (Genesis 2:2–3) ______________________________

Our ninth principle is: God rested. In turn, He tells us to rest. Disobedience to God's command to rest undoubtedly contributes to society's ills, including but not limited to workaholism, stress, chronic fatigue, emotional problems, and physical problems.

Undoubtedly our Creator established a day of rest because it's required if we're to be emotionally, physically, and spiritually fit. Are we modeling rest to our children so they have energy for the things God calls them to do? Might rest contribute to healthier family relationships? If we've not honored God's day of rest, is it too late to begin? No. We can start this week by responding to God's teachings and by starting to walk in His favor, health, and blessings.

Work Principle 10

5. Regardless of what kind of work we do, whom are we serving? (Colossians 3:24)

____

____

Our tenth principle is that our work is service to the Lord. We may not know why we're in what appears to be a dead-end job. However, consider Joseph in prison or Esther before she became queen. Wherever we are, let's be faithful to God in the midst of our situation.

Work Principle 11

Our eleventh principle is: God rewards those who work heartily for Him. The Bible is filled with references to God's rewards. It's a blessing to keep this verse in mind if you're passed up for a promotion or not given the pay raise for which you had hoped. We find comfort knowing God sees the good work we're doing and will reward us one day.

Work Principle 12

7. What can a slothful, disobedient, disrespectful, people-pleasing, insincere employee expect? (Colossians 3:25) ______________________________

Our twelfth principle is: those who do wrong will receive due consequences. Sometimes the consequences are immediate. Other times, they're delayed. Regardless, God warns us that wrongdoers will suffer consequences.

Work Principle 13

8. Although the Bible is clear that we're to work, what high calling has God given believers? Fill in the blanks.

   a) John 6:27 "Do not work for the food which perishes, but for the food which endures to ________________ ________________, which the Son of Man will give to you, for on Him the Father, God, has set His seal."

   b) Ephesians 2:10 "For we are His workmanship, created in Christ Jesus for ________________ ________________, which God prepared beforehand so that we would walk in them."

Our thirteenth principle is: we're to work for that which endures to eternal life. In other words, God has given us work to do beyond bringing home the milk and bread. He's given us *eternal* work to do. We'll experience great joy and satisfaction when we walk in the good works He's given us to do.

Work Principle 14

9. What two words characterize how employers treat employees? (Colossians 4:1) ________________ and ________________.

Our fourteenth point is: employers are to treat employees with justice and fairness.

10. How are Christian employers who do this a witness? ________________

____

____

____

Work Principle 15

11. As we work heartily unto the Lord, who does Philippians 2:13 state is working in us? Fill in the blanks.

    "For it is ________________ who is at work in you, both to will and to work for His good pleasure."

God is at work. He's working in you right now through this study. Let's respond by bringing honor to Him in all we do.

What's in Your Basket?

Basket Case

- Not completed what God's called me to do
- Work 24/7—exhausted
- Resentful
- Not mindful am serving Lord
- Not serving the Lord; not doing anything of eternal value
- Unfair to employees

Extraordinary Life

- Am completing what God's called me to do
- Get needed rest; try to keep Sunday set apart
- Don't like my job
- Mindful am serving Lord
- Walking in good works God prepared for me to do
- Fair to employees

♦ *Perhaps I'm a basket case because I've not completed the work God's given me to do.*

♦ *Perhaps I'm a basket case because I don't rest. I'm exhausted.*

♦ *Perhaps I'm a basket case because I don't like my boss or job.*

♦ *Perhaps I'm a basket case because I'm not doing anything of eternal value. Life is an empty, meaningless treadmill. I need to plug into a ministry and serve God. I need to walk in the good works God's prepared for me to do.*

♦ *Perhaps I'm a basket case because I haven't treated my employees or children fairly.*

Thinking It Over

♥ 1. How do you feel about God's teaching that if someone doesn't work, then he shouldn't eat? ______________________________

____

____

♥ 2. Why do you think God set apart a day for you to rest? What happens when you don't get enough rest? How does it affect your family and work or church relationships and responsibilities? ______________________________

____

____

♥ 3. How is God working in you? Which principle from today's study do you want to remember? Why? ______________________________

____

____

Day 3: *Devote Yourself to Prayer*

Father, speak to my heart through Your Word today. Teach me to recognize and follow Your voice. Help me become a faithful prayer warrior. I love You. In Jesus's name. Amen.

◆ ◆ ◆

Mary watched her mother close the door as she quietly slipped outside. Her mother had always been the first to rise each morning, but Mary had never thought much about it. She assumed she was getting an early start on breakfast. Now she realized her mother was doing something before she began breakfast. She was praying. Mary then noticed other times her mother prayed. When her brother was going through a difficult time, her mother could be found on her knees. When Mary shared with her mother her concern for Rachel, her mother didn't speak badly about Rachel. Instead, she suggested they pray for her. When a friend came over and shared a need, her mother would pray, and continue to pray, even after the friend had left. When Mary and her dad had a disagreement, her mother would slip away to pray. "Help me be more devoted to prayer, Lord," Mary whispered to God.

◆ ◆ ◆

Paul loved the Lord! He loved how the Lord Jesus, His Savior, wasn't a far-removed God. Rather, He was with Paul. Paul sensed His presence. Paul rejoiced that he could talk with God day or night. Christ was Paul's first thought in the morning. During the day, He guided Paul. Paul took his joys, worries, fears, and frustrations to the Lord Jesus, who inspired Paul with hope, perspective, calm, and patience. "Good morning, Lord," Paul prayed, as he quieted himself to sense God speaking to his mind, his heart.

◆ ◆ ◆

Read Colossians 4:2–4.

Prayer Principle 1 We Are to Devote *Ourselves to Prayer*

Devote comes from a word that means "be steadfastly attentive to, continue in, persevere, be in constant readiness for one."

1. Why do you think Christians are to devote themselves to prayer? ________________

____

2. What happens when you don't pray? ________________________________

____

3. What happens when you pray? ________________________________

____

Prayer Principle 2 We Are to Keep Alert *in Prayer*

Alert is a powerful word! Here, it means "to watch, give strict attention to, take heed lest through remission some destructive calamity suddenly overtake us." If that doesn't motivate us to pray, I don't know what will!

4. How do the following Scriptures support Paul's statement? ______________

   1 Peter 5:8 ____

   Matthew 26:41 ______________________________________

Prayer should be a priority for us also because of the reality of spiritual warfare. The devil's aim is to hurt believers emotionally, physically, and spiritually—to destroy the believer. If we are wise and listen to Christ's teaching, as well as the Apostle Paul's words of warning, we will make prayer our priority and remain alert.

5. Check the following areas where Satan tempts you.

   - ❑ food
   - ❑ unwholesome thoughts
   - ❑ money
   - ❑ gambling
   - ❑ depression
   - ❑ competitiveness
   - ❑ negativity
   - ❑ procrastination
   - ❑ self-pity
   - ❑ control, power
   - ❑ work
   - ❑ pornography
   - ❑ loneliness
   - ❑ blame
   - ❑ hopelessness
   - ❑ worry
   - ❑ jealousy
   - ❑ possessions
   - ❑ pride
   - ❑ alcohol, drugs
   - ❑ anger/bitterness
   - ❑ lying
   - ❑ strife
   - ❑ television

God warns us to keep alert to what's going on in and around us. When we feel depressed, anxious, or apathetic, or critical about ourselves or others, we need to "Stop, Drop, and P.R.A.Y." as explained in *Pray with Purpose, Live with Passion.*

Prayer Principle 3 We Are to Pray with an Attitude... of Thanks

Have you ever said of someone, "He's got an attitude!"? Or said, "You need a better attitude!"? *Thanksgiving* means "thankfulness." If we can see other's attitudes, don't we realize that God sees ours?

6. How do you think it makes God feel when you pray with an ungrateful attitude?

____

____

7. Which of the following has entered your thoughts while praying?
   - ❑ *I don't know if You're listening, God. My needs aren't as important as others.*
   - ❑ *If You're listening, God, You probably won't do what I'm asking, but just in case…*
   - ❑ *I don't know why I'm praying. It never does any good.*

Recently, I walked out onto my front porch and heard the loudest tweeting I've ever heard. I expected to see a gigantic bird and watched for the branches to rustle so I could spot the happy caroler. Instead, my eyes fell on a tiny little bird. It was the cutest thing I'd ever seen. It was stretching and straining, causing the bough to bend up and down. As I listened and found pleasure watching that little bird, I thought about how much pleasure my heavenly Father must have when we stretch our arms heavenward and praise Him. Does God see us? Of course He does! Does God note the one who joyfully comes to Him thanking Him for answered prayer? Yes!

Another day recently, I was so joyful that I was about to burst. I fell on my knees and simply smiled and thanked God repeatedly for what He was doing.

A negative question from a negative-thinking loved one or co-worker doesn't engage us in the way a positive question from a thankful person does. For instance, there have been times when Keith has asked me to do something I didn't want to do, but I couldn't resist his boyish grin or playful big brown eyes.

What does God see when you call on Him? A sullen, doubting saint or an expectant, hopeful child?

There *are* times when we go to God with broken hearts and broken dreams. There *are* times when we're miserably sick, worried, or despairing. Does praying with thanksgiving mean we're to fake it with God or pretend happiness? No.

8. Look up the following verses and record what they say about mourning.

   a) Matthew 5:4 ______________________________

   b) John 11:32–35 ______________________________

   c) What accompanied Jesus's tears? (John 11:41) ____________________

   d) James 4:9 ______________________________

Ecclesiastes 3:4 tells us that there's "a time to weep and a time to laugh, a time to mourn and a time to dance." Jesus states that He will bless those who mourn. He wept when Lazarus died. However, He also models praying with thanksgiving, which is what we're instructed to do.

Thanksgiving is related to hope. When we pray, we're to have an attitude of hope, not based on our goodness, but rather on God's grace. Our hope is in God, who attends to our prayers, is merciful, and answers our prayers according to His will. Approach God's throne with boldness, dear sisters. Your loving Father awaits you! And remember to sing praises to Him for prayers He's answering!

Prayer Principle 4 We Are to Pray for Others

9. Reread Colossians 4:3. Who asked for prayer?
   ❑ Paul ❑ Timothy

10. I know some people seldom ask for prayer for themselves. If you know someone like that, what is his or her reasoning? ______________________________

____

I'm sorry for Christians who miss the blessing of Christ's body of prayer warriors. Since writing our study today, I called a friend God placed on my heart to see how she's doing. As we talked, God revealed how I could pray for this powerful saint! As I checked emails, I prayed for those on our church prayerline. Later, my phone beeped reminders to pray for two sisters having surgery, one at 8:00 A.M. and one at 11:00 A.M. It was an honor to lift them in prayer. Another friend called with a praise report for their child who has overcome a smoking and drinking problem. I rejoiced with that sister. Another sister called asking for prayer for a child going to a job interview. As I knelt and prayed, I thought of how many people had prayed for my children through the years and what a blessing it is to pray for theirs.

11. Do you have family and/or sisters in Christ with whom you pray? If not, why? If you do, what's your testimony regarding the privilege of praying for one another and the power of intercessory prayer? ______________________________

____

We can ask others to pray for us. Jesus asked for prayer for Himself. The Apostle Paul followed Jesus's example and asked for others to pray for him.

You don't have to expose details about yourself or your loved ones. General prayer requests can be made without exposing personal details. For example, a person who is prone to addictions, can ask for prayer simply by asking others to pray for their physical, emotional, and spiritual health. If your husband had an affair, you can ask for prayer for God to guide your steps and guard your emotions. We can take advantage of the blessing of having other believers pray for us. We don't have to fight our battles alone.

12. For what would you like prayer? ______________________________

Pray for that request with an attitude of thanksgiving. Rest assured God is looking lovingly on you.

Prayer Principle 5 We're to Pray for God to Open Doors *for the Word*

This exciting prayer request is in keeping with Jesus's mission: to seek and save the lost (Luke 19:10).

13. For what did Paul ask? ____________________________

14. What did Paul want to do? (Colossians 4:3) ____________________

Paul didn't ask others to pray that God would open his prison doors so he could be free. He humbly asked God to open a door of opportunity for them to speak the Word!

Did God answer their humble prayer? Yes! Was God's eye on His servant? Yes! And His eye is on you and His ear is open to you. What's your heart? Are you passionate to serve Christ, to let others know God will help them as He helped you, that He'll forgive their sins as He's forgiven you?

15. What happens when we become a part of not only praying for health and jobs but also praying for people to turn to God and be saved? What emotion do we share with the angels in heaven when that prayer is answered? (Luke 15:7)

____

____

The best antidote to self-pity and despair is to join Christ's kingdom work. When despair blows in like a cold north wind, when anger boils within like an erupting volcano, we know what to do. As children of the King, we can grab hold of those emotions and put them in time-out before our Father in heaven. We can speak directly to the Lord about what's going on in our hearts and minds. We must be alert to Satan, who is always seeking to destroy us. We can be wise and contemplate what Christ is teaching us in our situations. Is a wave of despair a test? We can practice thanksgiving! Is the devil inviting us to a pity party? Just say no! The antidote to being down and out is to look up and P.R.A.Y. (Praise! Repent! Ask! Yield!) Set your mind on the things above. And join the kingdom's salvation prayer team. Begin praying for the unsaved.

16. What is Paul's specific prayer request? I am in love with his humble soul! (Colossians 4:4) ____________________________________

____

Paul's request is to be "clear in the way I ought to speak." He's asking what to say as he shares Christ. Colossians 4:4 and 1 Corinthians 2:2–5 are my prayer requests as I teach Bible studies and lead conferences and retreats. A group of precious saints prays for me. They are as much a part of my ministry as my teaching!

If you're not a Christian, God invites you to say the most important prayer of your life:

> "I'm sorry. I know I'm a sinner. I know I've fallen short of Your holiness. Please forgive me. I repent. I turn to You as my Lord and Savior. Today I am believing in Christ for eternal life. Thank You for forgiving and saving me. I love You, Lord. In Jesus's name. Amen."

What's in Your Basket?

Basket Case

- Don't ask for prayer
- Sometimes pray for others
- Praying for others
- Forget the prayers God's answered
- When tempted or dejected, don't consider what God's teaching me or how He wants me to grow

Extraordinary Life

- Devoted to prayer; alert in prayer
- Seeing God answer prayer
- Express thanks to God
- Engaged in prayer for the unsaved
- Pray for God to open doors for me to share Christ

♦ *Perhaps I'm a basket case because I haven't grasped the joy of prayer, of being part of something eternal.*

♦ *Perhaps I'm a basket case because when I get down, I don't consider what God's trying to teach me.*

♦ *Perhaps I'm a basket case because I don't stay alert in prayer.*

♦ *Perhaps I'm a basket case because I'm not engaged in praying for others.*

♦ *Perhaps I'm a basket case because I don't record my prayers and recognize how God's answering them. (If this is your situation, I invite you to begin using my prayer journal, Prayers of My Heart.)*

Thinking It Over

♥ 1. How is God speaking to you about your prayer life?

____

____

____

♥ 2. What points do you want to remember from today's study?

____

____

____

♥ 3. How is God leading you to pray?

____

____

____

____

Day 4: *Make the Most of Every Opportunity*

Father, I love You and praise You for the privilege of knowing You, of having Your Word, and for the gift of the Holy Spirit. Help me communicate Your love, joy, hope, and salvation to those who don't know You. In Jesus's name. Amen.

◆ ◆ ◆

Mary prayed for the right moment to talk to Rachel about Jesus. They had talked around their different beliefs for a year. Mary was now convicted that it was time for a direct conversation. "There's a time when you must speak up. If you truly care about someone, you'll respectfully ask them about their faith," her father explained.

◆ ◆ ◆

Paul rose from his knees and hugged the big burly guard who had just prayed to receive Christ. "My sins are washed away? I'm forgiven? Are you sure, Paul?" "I'm sure," Paul answered.

◆ ◆ ◆

Read Colossians 4:5–6.

I've been anxiously *waiting* for us to get to these verses. I've saved articles, pulled books from my bookcases, and been amazed as God has provided resources to share with you. It's been a joy to watch God's divine hand prepare the teachings for this and the previous week's segment. It is my prayer that you embrace each Scripture and hide each biblical truth in your heart.

Today's Scriptures are vital because they focus on why Christ came to earth and died for our sins. They direct us to our part in God's kingdom plan. First, let me share with you a story to prepare us for today's study.

Years ago, Keith wanted a new reading lamp. Because his eyesight is poor, this was really important. Due to his busy schedule, he didn't have time to go lamp shopping, plus, he's not a shopper. I made sporadic attempts to find him a lamp, but couldn't find the right one. In the meantime, he sat in the dark and used the lamp he already had, inadequate as it was. I resolved numerous times to find him a lamp, but never actually did so.

Are any of you thinking, *Well, you would think Debbie would take time to find Keith a lamp?*

Let me tell you another story. People are sitting in spiritual darkness. They're spiritually blind. They're trying to make their way through life. Many of them don't have time to seek out our churches. Even if they did, they wouldn't go church shopping. We may have made some attempt to mention Christ to them, but we haven't made it a top priority. We've waited for the perfect words and time and simply haven't followed through. I wonder what Christ thinks about that?

Today we're studying biblical principles about sharing our faith, an important part of our Christian responsibility.

Sharing Principle 1

God wants Christians to share Christ with non-Christians.

1. What is on Paul's heart continually, which is the reason for his imprisonment? (Colossians 4:3–4) ____________________

____

2. Has your prayer ever been, "God, open a door for me to speak to someone about Christ"? ____________________

____

3. Although not everyone is called to missions in another country, what two things are believers instructed to do? (Colossians 4:5) Answer in the first person: replace *yourselves* with *myself.*

   a) ____________________

   b) ____________________

We're to be continually mindful of conducting ourselves with wisdom toward unbelievers. We're to make every opportunity to share Christ.

Some Christians say they don't speak of Christ to others because they don't want to push their faith on people. I would remind them that Christ commands us to go and teach others about Him; baptizing them in His name. Jesus said we're to go and "make disciples." The command isn't to a select few, but to all believers. It requires talking as well as living a godly life.

4. Look up Matthew 28:18–20. Check the following true statements.
   - ❑ Jesus says He's the heavenly and worldly authority. (v. 18)
   - ❑ Jesus commands the world be evangelized according to His message of salvation by faith in Him. (v. 19)
   - ❑ Jesus commands Christians to go and teach His commandments to all nations; and to baptize all nations in His name. (v. 19)
   - ❑ Jesus says there are many ways to heaven.

We have to contemplate what Jesus commands. Did Jesus not know other people had other faiths? Of course He did. Did Jesus not know other people followed prophets other than Him? Yes, He knew. Then is the Jewish Savior from Nazareth a little off? Or, is He who the Bible says He is: God?

How are we to reckon Christ's theology with the world's theology that everyone can choose their own path to heaven? How do we reconcile Christ's teachings with today's theology that says everyone worships the same god; he simply has different names?

Was Jesus wrong when He said all nations are to be baptized in *His* name?

5. Place a check beside the nations and people God had an impact on, on the day He sent the Holy Spirit (Acts 2:4–11).

❑ Arabs	❑ Asia	❑ Cappadocia	❑ Cretans	❑ Cyrene	❑ Egypt
❑ Elamites	❑ Judea	❑ Libya	❑ Medes	❑ Mesopotamia	❑ Pamphylia
❑ Parthians	❑ Phrygia	❑ Pontus	❑ Rome		

There are different perspectives regarding religions other than Christianity. However, Christ's words are true words. Consider the following words by Al-Gharib who was born and raised in an Arab-Muslim country. His father named him after the prophet Muhammad. Al-Gharib outwardly professed conversion to Christianity, but then faced confusion. He later came to know Jesus Christ as His Savior. Part of his story is below.

> Within a three-day period of reading the Holy Scriptures in the light and with the guidance of the Holy Spirit I was able to discover many of the answers I was looking for (i.e. the Trinity, the Deity of Jesus, his crucifixion, resurrection). Furthermore, the Holy Spirit extended my spiritual sight to see beyond the natural realm like discerning about time and sights. Regarding Islam, I discovered overwhelming biblical prophecies that were bitter for me to swallow. The most shocking answer I received was about Allah. He is not God "Yhwh" of the Bible, but someone else.
>
> (To read his full testimony, go to www.answering-islam.org/Testimonies/algharib.html.)

Sharing Principle 2

Christians are to conduct themselves with wisdom toward non-Christians.

6. Was Jesus wrong to say all nations are to be baptized in His name? Or are we wrong to not pray as Paul did for God to open doors of opportunity for us to share Christ with those living in spiritual darkness?

   ❑ Jesus was wrong. ❑ I've been wrong.

Christ's message isn't only for people of other major religions. It's for our neighbors who follow humanist spiritual teachings rather than Christ. It's for anyone who doesn't know Christ as Savior.

7. How does Paul instruct Christians to conduct themselves? (Colossians 4:5)

____

____

8. Why is it important to conduct yourself with wisdom toward unbelievers?

____

____

In regard to this principle, I've messed up on many occasions. Whether in college or a month ago, I often fail to conduct myself with wisdom. In Al-Gharib's testimony, he shares the following about a wise nun and a foolish nun. I believe this illustrates Paul's point about the need for us to conduct ourselves with wisdom.

> The wise nun: When I was a baby I got a dangerous sickness and my mother had to leave me in the hospital for three days in the intensive care unit. The nurse who was in charge of me was a Catholic nun. When I became a boy my father told me several times: "That nun saved your life." I never understood what he said and why until years later. When I became a Christian, the story came back to my memory and I understood what my father's message was. When I was struggling between life and death in that nun's hands, she prayed for me and the Lord answered her. I owe that nun my life and I am so thankful for her gift of prayer and love.
>
> The foolish nun: When I was a teenager, my mother got very sick and had to stay in the hospital (another one) that was under the supervision of a Catholic nun. Technically, she was a hard working nun but had what seemed to be little compassion or respect toward anyone. Everybody hated her because of her meanness. Regardless of her many good works, I believe that her lack of love toward people destroyed her true ministry and she misrepresented Christ. I still have a bad memory of her and I find it hard to forgive her still.

9. What about you? Have you ever spoken or acted in a way that didn't reflect properly on Christ?

   ❑ Yes ❑ No

If you answered yes, you can join me at His footstool in repentance! Jesus is waiting for us with arms open wide.

Sharing Principle 3

Make the most of any opportunity to share Christ.

Reread Colossians 4:5.

This is such sound advice. We don't have to look far to find unbelieving friends, family, work associates. Whether it's someone with whom you work or live, ask God to open doors for you to share Christ.

10. Paul's warning is a good word to us. Do you have an unbelieving son, daughter, friend, or co-worker? What is Paul saying? Check all that are true. (Colossians 4:5)
    - ❑ My conduct with unbelievers isn't important to Christ's kingdom.
    - ❑ My conduct can have a favorable or unfavorable impression.
    - ❑ I should make the most of every opportunity to share Christ.
    - ❑ It's OK for me not to make the most of every opportunity to share Christ because I'm shy.

Sharing Principle 4

My speech should be seasoned with grace and salt.

11. Colossians 4:6 is a great verse to memorize regarding our speech. Reread it, then fill in the blanks below.

    "Let your speech ________________ be with ________________, as though seasoned with salt, so that you will know how you should respond to each person.

I was tickled to death one Sunday when Taylor was in town and started asking me hard questions about what happens to the person who never hears Jesus's name. "Will that person be saved?" We'd discussed this years ago, but the topic was fresh on Taylor's mind because he'd been discussing spiritual matters with a friend he's not sure is a Christian. Sitting around a campfire, on a hunt, after tennis, before a school meeting, while shopping—all these are opportune times to share Christ!

When we speak of Christ with others, we should always show the utmost respect. Paul explains that our words should be spoken with grace. This doesn't mean we put on our ballet shoes and dance around important subjects. It means we speak kindly, with goodwill.

12. What does 1 Peter 3:15 advise? Fill in the blanks with the following words: *conscience, gentleness, sanctify, defense.*

    a) ____________________ Christ as Lord in your hearts.

    b) Always be ready to make a ____________________ to everyone who asks you to give an account for the hope that is in you.

    c) Speak of Christ with others with ____________________ and reverence.

    d) Keep a good ____________________.

What's in Your Basket?

Basket Case

- Don't speak of Christ except to Christians
- Don't always conduct myself wisely
- Don't pray for or look for opportunities to share Christ
- Words seasoned, but not with grace

Extraordinary Life

- Speak of Christ to non-Christians
- Conduct myself with wisdom
- Pray for and make most of opportunities to share Christ
- Words seasoned with grace and salt

♦ *Perhaps I'm a basket case because I've been confused about my role with unbelievers.*

♦ *Perhaps I'm a basket case because I want to share Christ, but I don't pray for God to open doors.*

♦ *Perhaps I'm a basket case because I don't take advantage of opportunities God gives me to share Christ. I sit with my mouth closed; then feel bad for not speaking up.*

♦ *Perhaps I'm a basket case because when I do have an opportunity to talk about Christ, I'm unprepared. Then I tend to be blunt instead of gracious.*

♦ *Perhaps I'm a basket case because I want to share Christ but feel as though I've blown it with the unbeliever.*

Thinking It Over

♥ 1. Do you believe God wants you to share Christ with others? ____________________

♥ 2. If you could share one thing about what Christ means to you, what would it be?

____

____

♥ 3. Your relationship with Christ is a treasure. Why not ask God to provide an opportunity for you to share Christ with someone? This may be why you're in this study. God works in wonderful, surprising ways. Why not trust Him and pray right now for that door and opportunity? Then when He provides it, share what you wrote in question 2. Record your prayer asking God to open a door of opportunity.

____

____

Day 5: *Personal Remarks*

Lord God Almighty, You love me. You saved me. You've taught me. Now fill me and use me to spread Your love and Word to others. With love and thankfulness for all You've taught me in this study. In Jesus's name. Amen.

◆ ◆ ◆

Mary listened as Paul listed Christians who sent their greetings. It was good to know people had visited Paul while he was imprisoned. Mary couldn't wait for a full report from Tychicus and Onesimus! In the meantime, she breathed a prayer of thanks to God for her conversation with Rachel. Rachel had tired of looking for power in crystals. She tired of the visiting spiritists. Her heart was open to Jesus.

◆ ◆ ◆

Paul looked at the first golden rays of dawn streaking across the sky. He wished he could deliver the letter himself. "Lord, when will I be released? However, not my will, but Yours. If I can best serve You here, then I gladly do so."

◆ ◆ ◆

Read Colossians 4:7–18. You're going to love the "rest of the story" about these saints we'll discuss today!

1. Who is the first person Paul mentions in Colossians 4:7?

2. In what three ways does Paul refer to Tychicus?

   a) ______________________________

   b) ______________________________

   c) ______________________________

"Beloved brother," "faithful servant," "fellow bond-servant in the Lord." What incredible accolades this little-known saint received. No book of the Bible is named after Tychicus. He wasn't one of the 12 disciples, yet he found a place of service and was faithful to the Lord and fellow Christians. Not only was he faithful, he was loved. We've probably all known "hardworking" Christians who are not fun to be around. They have a scowl on their faces and are controlling. In other words, *love* isn't the first word that pops in your mind when their names are mentioned. However, *beloved* was Paul's first thought in relation to Tychicus.

Paul couldn't go to Colossae, so he sent his beloved friend.

3. What are two other points we learn about Tychicus? (I'm liking this saint more all the time!) (Colossians 4:8)

   a) ______________________________

   b) ______________________________

In addition to Tychicus being a beloved brother, faithful servant, and bond servant in the Lord, we discover he's trustworthy to convey information accurately. In addition, he's an encourager.

When I read about Tychicus, I immediately thought of Cynthia, our Hill Country Ministries administrator. She's not only our administrator, she's a great friend, sister in Christ, someone I can count on, and an incredible encourager!

4. Do we realize how precious each of these gifts are? Are you someone who can be counted on? Are you a bond servant of the Lord who works by another's side to accomplish God's goals? With whom do you work side by side to serve the Lord?

____

5. Who is someone in your life who is dependable, faithful to the Lord, and an encourager to you as you serve Him? ______________________________

Are you an encourager? Do you realize what a great gift that is? Today while writing, I received an email from a friend. It was a word of encouragement about how much our study has meant to her. My heart soared when I read her words. As a matter of fact, I reread, printed, and saved the email. It's precious to me that she took time to email me. God used this sister in my life today.

6. Would you not waste the God-given gift of encouragement if God has entrusted that gift to you? Who is someone you could encourage today? ____________________

7. Who accompanied Tychicus to Colossae? (Colossians 4:9) __________________

8. How does Paul refer to Onesimus? (Colossians 4:9)
   ❑ The runaway slave ❑ Our faithful and beloved brother

Who was Onesimus? He was a runaway slave. If you read the Book of Philemon, you'll discover Onesimus ran away from his master, Philemon. Many scholars think that he eventually made his way to Rome and while there, met Paul, who led him to Christ. Paul sent Onesimus back to his master, with the Colossian letter in hand, asking him to treat Onesimus with justice and fairness, reminding Philemon that he has a Master in heaven.

9. How did Paul ask Philemon to accept Onesimus when he returned? (Philemon 17)

____

____

10. What did Paul offer? (Philemon 18–19) ______________________________

____

____

I love that Paul told Philemon to charge to his account anything Onesimus owed. What an incredible picture of what Jesus does for us. He takes us while we're slaves of sin. He introduces us to God, who washes and saves us. He forgives our past and no longer calls us slaves, but rather, friends. He relates to us on the basis of our new identity in Christ. Our sins? They're charged to Jesus's account, paid in full on the Cross!

11. Who else is in Paul's friendship hall of fame? (Colossians 4:10–12)

____

____

Aristarchus, Paul's fellow prisoner, and Mark (with whom Paul once had conflict but became close) are included in his list. Finally, Justus rounds out the trio of Jews who accepted Jesus as the Christ and were encouragers to Paul. No doubt, they were men with whom he prayed.

Paul then mentions Epaphras, who evangelized Colossae, Hierapolis, and Laodicea. It was his report that prompted Paul to write the letter to the Colossae believers. Aren't we glad Epaphras shared his heart with Paul? Aren't we glad Paul committed every waking day to God?

12. What did Paul say about Epaphras? (Colossians 4:12–13) ________________

____

____

13. God uses believing bond servants like Epaphras, who in gratitude for their salvation give their lives to Jesus for Him to use. Are you such a believer?

    - ❑ Yes. I've presented my body as a living and holy sacrifice to Jesus. The life I now live I live because of my faith in Jesus Christ. (Romans 12:1–2)
    - ❑ I no longer live, but Christ lives in me. (Galatians 2:20)
    - ❑ My body is the temple of the Holy Spirit. I've been bought with Christ's blood. (1 Corinthians 6:19–20)
    - ❑ I seek to be daily, continually filled with Christ's Spirit. (Ephesians 5:18)
    - ❑ I walk by Christ's Spirit. (Galatians 5:16)
    - ❑ I bear the fruit of the Holy Spirit. (Galatians 5:22–23)
    - ❑ I fulfill the ministry of reconciliation Christ's entrusted to me. (2 Corinthians 5:18)
    - ❑ No. I'm saved, but have not committed my life to Jesus for Him to use for His kingdom. (If you haven't, would you like to now? It's the best life this side of heaven! Prayerfully review the above Scriptures and make them a part of your life.)

14. Paul mentions two other men. What does he say about each? (Colossians 4:14)

Man	**What Paul Says**
____________________	____
____________________	____

15. Did you notice Demas is the only person whom Paul says nothing about? There is no "beloved" attached to his name, no word about him being an encourager. The absence of accolades is like the absence of eternal rewards for Christians who live for themselves rather than Christ. If you'd like to find out more about Demas, read 2 Timothy 4:10.

What is sadly reported about Demas? ____

Dear sisters, "He loved this present world" is a sad epitaph. May it not be said of us.

16. Next Paul greets people in Colossae and Laodicea. What woman opened her home as a place for the church to meet?
❑ Ruth ❑ Nympha

How do you think this woman felt when Paul acknowledged her? I imagine it encouraged her! One day, sweet saint, you'll hear Jesus acknowledge you before His heavenly Father. All the hours of work, pain, tears, child-raising; being a conscientious employee, a faithful wife, a supportive daughter-in-law, or a caregiver will be rewarded when the Lord Jesus says your name.

17. In addition to Paul writing a letter to Colossae, to what other church did he write a letter? (Colossians 4:16) ____

No one knows what happened to the Laodicea letter. However, we know what happened to the church at Laodicea. They became lukewarm Christians. The risen Lord wanted to spit them out of his mouth (Revelation 3:14–22). They should have paid attention to God's warnings. Sound advice for us!

18. Record Paul's final parting words to Archippus and I believe to us. (Colossians 4:17)

____

____

____

19. Paul has poured out his heart. He has warned us not to follow spiritual paths that lead us away from pure devotion to Christ. He has reminded us Christ is all and

in all, the hope of glory. Paul has given us practical advice on parenting, family relationships, work, and sharing our faith. In return, what simple request does Paul make? (Colossians 4:18) ______________________________

____

I believe Paul would want us to remember our brothers and sisters in prison. The article on page 218, "Boy slave 'crucified' by Sudanese Muslim," reminds us that many throughout the world are suffering for Christ. Let us remember them in our prayers.

20. How does Paul close? (Colossians 4:18) ______________________________

____

____

Sisters, it's been a blessing studying through Colossians with you. Thank you for the time and energy you put into your study. I close as did Paul, with the heartfelt words, "Grace to you," and look forward to our next time together.

What's in Your Basket?

Basket Case

- Think about encouraging others but don't often get around to it
- Saved
- Love the world more than serving Christ and His body, the church
- Stop short rather than fulfill what God's given me to do
- Treat people on the basis of their past, not their new identity in Christ

Extraordinary Life

- Encourage others often
- Am Christ's bond servant
- Love my fellow sisters and brothers in Christ
- Fulfill my ministry; do whatever I can for the kingdom
- Treat people on the basis of their identity in Christ, not their past

♦ *Perhaps I'm a basket case because I'm saved but don't approach each day as Christ's bond servant.*

♦ *Perhaps I'm a basket case because I love the world more than the Creator of the world.*

♦ *Perhaps I'm a basket case because I seek encouragement but don't give it.*

♦ *Perhaps I'm a basket case because I haven't guarded the ministry God's given me; whether it's raising children, being a godly wife, leading a Bible study, or being a faithful witness at work. I tend to complain and want to quit.*

♦ *Perhaps I'm a basket case because I don't treat people on the basis of their new identity in Christ. I treat them on the basis of their past wrongs.*

Thinking It Over

♥ 1. How is God speaking to you through today's study? What golden nugget do you want to remember? ______________________________

♥ 2. What is your prayer in relation to how God has spoken to you?

The Following Can Be Answered for Today's Discussion or Later for Share Day

♥ 3. Flip through the pages of Colossians. As you think about all we've studied, what golden nuggets do you want most to remember? ______________________________

♥ 4. What golden nugget do you need to immediately act on? ______________________________

♥ 5. What verses have meant the most to you? Which have you hidden in your heart?

♥ 6. Will you thank Jesus for how He's spoken to you, then go and tell someone God is speaking if only we'll listen? Invite them to our next study.

Blessings to you as you live an extraordinary life for our Lord Jesus.

Love, Debbie

Weekly Wrap-Up

Where Am I? With which basket-case point do I most relate?

Where Do I Want to Be? To which aspects of extraordinary living is God calling me?

How Will I Get There? What golden nugget and/or verse do I want to remember to help me better handle my basket-case moments and live an extraordinary life?

Thinking of Others: What from this week's study do I want to share with someone to encourage or warn them?

WorldNET Daily

FAITH UNDER FIRE

Boy slave 'crucified' by Sudanese Muslim

Now a youth, he tells Voice of the Martyrs he's forgiven attacker

Posted: September 28, 2006

1:00 A.M. Eastern

© 2006 WorldNetDaily.com

—A Sudanese slave who was assigned to watch his Muslim master's camels was "crucified" when he was caught sneaking out to attend a Christian church, according to reports from Voice of the Martyrs . . . .

Damare Garang was seven when the attack happened, officials said. He had been captured by Islamic soldiers when his Sudanese village was attacked, and then sold as a slave to a Muslim family in Tuobon, Bahr el Gazel.

His duties were to tend the master's camels, but one day fled.

"How could you do this? You will surely have to pay! You stupid slave, I should just kill you now," he was told.

However, the child escaped any injuries at that point.

Then the following day Damare, who had been raised in a Christian family, sneaked away for a time to a small church service across the village.

His master was waiting when he returned.

"Where have you been?" he was asked, and partly from fear and partly from not having another answer, he said, "to church."

"You have made two grave mistakes," the slave master said. "Yesterday you lost one of my camels, and today you worship with infidels!"

The master went to a barn and returned with a large board, some rusty spikes and a hammer, the report said.

"Frozen in fear, Damare was dragged out to the edge of his master's compound where he was forced to the ground with his legs over the board," the VOM report said. "The savage brutality of the master was unleashed as he proceeded to drive the long nails through Damare's knees and then nail his feet securely onto the board."

While Damare was screaming in agony, the slave master simply walked away.

The boy's help arrived in the form of a Good Samaritan who happened by, and saw the small boy. The man sneaked into the compound and carried the boy to a hospital where the board and nails were removed.

Damare later was released to the custody of his helper, with whom he lived for the next 18 months.

Once again, then, there was a militia attack on his village, and he was separated from his protector. When the Islamic army soldiers were driven off, a commander of village forces recognized Damare's speech as being of the Dinka tribe, and took charge of him.

That commander eventually adopted Damare, who now lives in Mario Kong.

He remains disappointed he is unable to run quickly like other boys, but he says he's forgiven his attacker, because Jesus was nailed to a cross to forgive all sins....

"Please tell the Christian children in America to remember to pray for the children of Sudan," Damare told his visitors.

TIPS FOR LEADERS

Dear Leaders:

Thank you for leading the discussion for *If God Is in Control, Why Am I a Basket Case?* You're in my hero hall of fame! I know each of you probably has a full plate of responsibilities of family, work, church, and other ministry commitments. Yet, you've responded to God's call to help others grow closer to our Lord! I commend each of you and will be praying for you. As a matter of fact, may I pray for you right now?

> Heavenly Father, You are an awesome God! We stand amazed in Your presence. You equip us to do what we're unable to accomplish in our own strength. You empower us to serve You. Thank You for these dear sisters who've committed their lives and time to You. Fill and anoint them with Your Spirit. Guard them from the enemy. Give them a special taste of Your heavenly Word each day as they study and prepare to lead their groups. As Jesus lived an extraordinary life that pointed others to You, may each leader do so also. In Jesus's name. Amen.

Now down to the basics! I've led small-group discussions and know how rewarding, yet how challenging they can be. If you don't already have *A Leader's Heart* manual, in which I give tips for leading a small-group study, I encourage you to get a copy. In relation to this study, keep the following tips in mind.

1. If you have experience leading a discussion group, you're aware some people like short studies while others like longer, in-depth studies. The solution? Suggest to your group if they don't have time to read all of the comments on Bible passages, simply to answer the questions. For those who want more study, encourage them to read the comments as well as look up the additional verses referenced.

2. Encourage your group to memorize verses, but don't force it. Some people have memory problems and can't memorize. Others will soar at the opportunity to memorize Scripture. *Your* zeal for memorizing God's Word will be the most contagious way to motivate others to memorize it.

3. Your enthusiasm for the study is contagious. Stay in touch with your group each week. Encourage them to complete their lessons and to attend. A simple email, such

as "I loved today's lesson! Isn't Colossians 3:2–3 applicable to us today? See you at class!" will let your group know you're thinking about them.

4. At the end of each day's study, you'll find "Basket Case/Extraordinary Life" and "Thinking It Over" questions and statements. If you wish, these can be used for group discussion in conjunction with the daily questions your group will enjoy discussing. In addition, there are "Weekly Wrap-Up" questions that can be used for group discussion. Any of these or a combination can be used to lead your discussion.

5. Preparation is *key* to leading a good discussion, Prayerfully plan your group time by asking someone to be a timekeeper or by setting the time and writing it next to each point you will cover in your discussion group. For instance, if your group begins at 9:00, you might follow the time guideline below.

   8:45 A.M. Group members arrive and visit.
   9:00 A.M Welcome and brief opening prayer.
   9:02 A.M Day 1
   9:15 A.M Day 2

6. Begin and end your group discussions on time. Leading your group in a timely manner shows respect for those who may be on tight schedules.

7. Enjoy your group! God has brought each person to the study. Arrive early so you're not rushed and can welcome each person as she arrives. Set up only the number of chairs for those in attendance. After all the members arrive, have someone remove unused chairs so your group can sit close together without empty or "cold" spots. Then, sit back and enjoy hearing what your group is learning. Aim for your group to have genuine discussion as they would with friends over lunch.

8. Pray, pray, pray. Satan gets his feathers ruffled when we study God's Word and grow. Living an extraordinary life for Christ may rouse the prowling lion. If you feel stressed and your basket-case moments seem to increase, praise God and practice what He's teaching you. He will strengthen you as you serve Him.

   Pray daily for your group. Someone might wonder what difference an eight-week study can make in someone's life. However, one point of application, one memorized verse, or one prayer can change a person's life.

9. Keep your eyes and heart open for the one who may not know Christ as Savior. At the end of the last day of our pilot study, a woman approached me and shared she wasn't sure she was a Christian. Imagine the joy we shared as she prayed to receive Christ as her Savior. Invite unsaved friends. You may be leading this study for such a time as this. Know I'm praying for you.

"Beyond all these things put on love, which is the perfect bond of unity."
—Colossians 3:14

New Hope® Publishers is a division of WMU®, an international organization that challenges Christian believers to understand and be radically involved in God's mission. For more information about WMU, go to www.wmu.com. More information about New Hope books may be found at www.newhopedigital.com. New Hope books may be purchased at your local bookstore.

Use the QR reader on your
smartphone to visit us online at
www.newhopedigital.com

If you've been blessed by this book, we would like to hear your story.
The publisher and author welcome your comments and
suggestions at: newhopereader@wmu.org.